Brand Triad

✦

Toolbox for Strategic Brand Assessment and Repositioning

Bill Nissim

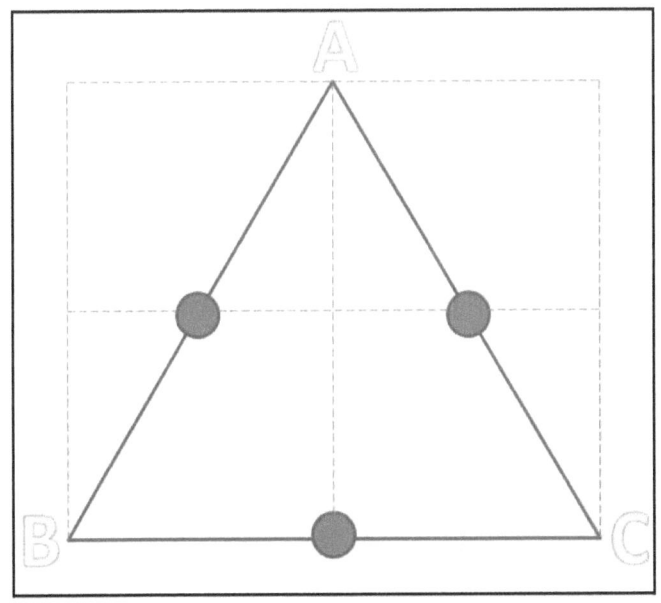

iUniverse, Inc.
New York   Bloomington

Brand Triad

Toolbox for Strategic Brand Assessment and Repositioning

iUniverse books may be ordered through booksellers or by contacting:

iUniverse
1663 Liberty Drive
Bloomington, IN 47403
www.iuniverse.com
1-800-Authors (1-800-288-4677)

ISBN: 978-0-595-52584-3 (pbk)
ISBN: 978-0-595-51355-0 (cloth)
ISBN: 978-0-595-62638-0 (ebk)

Printed in the United States of America

Preface

Shivering on the bridge of an ocean-faring catamaran, my eyes were transfixed by the dense cloud cover that had settled over the Southern California coastline. My gaze drifted from the looming fog bank ahead to a faint movement in the adjacent pilot house. Through a side glass window, the captain was eyeing an array of navigational equipment to guide our 134-foot tourist ship safely through the harbor. Minutes passed as our lumbering vessel traversed the channel's many twists and turns until it finally emerged through a pair of rocky jetties and into the vast Pacific Ocean. As our ship slipped into the luminous white haze, I noticed the coastline behind us had gradually disappeared from sight. Now, as our vessel was entirely engulfed by the fog, the coastal noise faded away and was replaced by an eerie silence; only the faint, rhythmic lapping of waves against our bow was audible. I glanced up and noticed three sets of waveguide arrays inconspicuously rotating on top of the pilot house. In the deafening silence of the open sea, I felt assured we would have a safe passage to our destination twenty-six miles away because our experienced crew was using the technology employed overhead.

In today's world, our reliance on technology has become ever increasing. In the case of our tourist ship, these were necessary tools to help make a series of navigational decisions. The advent of electronics, however, was not always a factor. Great journeys throughout our global history were undertaken as long as man sought to challenge the open seas; just think of Columbus, Magellan, and Ponce De Leon to name a few. How did these mariners of old confront and navigate the oceans successfully?

The most common tool applied by navigators was the use of our star system. If you were to gaze into the nighttime sky, you would notice an array of stars rising and falling on the horizon. There are, in fact, thirty-two points in the sky that navigators have used as a reference to guide their journeys. For every one of these stars that resides on the bow of a ship, a corresponding star lies directly at the stern. An imaginary line connects the two points with the vessel centered in the middle. For example, the opposite of the star Vega rising in the northeast is the setting of Antares in the southwest (Peter Ifland, 1998). In this manner, the technology employed by ancient mariners was a celestial map that provided directional information: north, south, east, and west, and every point in between.

In addition to direction, another tool was required to ascertain a ship's latitude: the ability to determine a position from the equator. The North Star, or Polaris, was the metric by which latitude could be assessed. For example, if you left port and Polaris was thirty-four degrees altitude from the horizon and you sailed north, the measured altitude of the North Star from the horizon would increase. Conversely, to return to your point of origin, you would merely head south until Polaris' altitude returned to thirty-four degrees, and then you would sail west or east depending on your starting point.

If the visual tool was the heavens, what physical device was employed to navigate the seven seas? In ancient times, mariners used the star map and their outstretched arm and fingers to sight the angle (latitude) from the horizon. This primal approach spawned a myriad of instruments from the most rudimentary of mechanical engines to the highly complex. The first of these was the quadrant, then the astrolabe, and later the sextant. Each subsequent device offered more features and provided greater ease of use. These devices evolved from handheld instruments constructed of wood and brass that used the stars, sun, and moon to sight their location to sophisticated GPS devices of today that rely on the triangulation of three or more satellites to denote location within 10 feet or less. How does maritime navigation relate to the topic of this book?

At first blush, its primary usefulness is symbolic and analogous to plotting a future course. In addition, the landscape of business practices has also evolved in much the same manner as marine navigation. The tools of commerce have progressed from simple exchanges—barter for goods—to sophisticated transactions such as reverse auctions which require complex Internet-based software to track and update bids. Another parallel includes uncontrollable events; whether a sudden storm, an unforeseen socioeconomic event, or disruptive technology, they are subject to confront these situations with only tools and wisdom to guide them.

In the realm of branding, this practice has existed in many forms over time and has only recently, in the twentieth century, received definition and its own methodology. In ancient times, a retailer would merely hang a sign on the door, which plainly stated their craft. For the benefit of the illiterate, symbols, or brands, were often used to convey expertise and wares to the masses. Although many captains of industry unknowingly applied branding principles, the concept wasn't established until Rosser Reeves (1961) synthesized it and labeled it USP (Unique Sales Proposition). Over the last four decades, the development of the branding concept has emerged from simple ideas to complex business models. As noted in Martin Lindstrom's book *Brand Sense*, this discipline has transitioned over the decades from USP to ESP (Emotional Selling), to OSP (Organizational Selling), to BSP (Brand Selling), and to today's MSP (Me Selling Proposition). Lindstrom espouses that there is a more sophisticated realm called HSP (Holistic Selling proposition) which emerges from traditions and rituals.

Another twenty-first century author usurps common branding methodologies and proposes that cultural dynamics determine a brand's relevance. In an era where viral, emotional, and mind share techniques are viewed as mainstream models, Douglas Holt applies case studies to recast our thinking to include the power of cultural tension and the opportunity to provide societal relief through brands. Holt defines his theory as iconic brands (2005).

Great brands are now being defined and critiqued by the model or process that influenced their success. As brands rise from obscurity to prominence, the artisan who crafted the ad campaign, brand strategy, or creative work attempts to credit their success to a specific methodology. The brand triad explores models developed in the past and offers new concepts for you to consider. The goal is to provide the marketing practitioner, or brand advocate, the full spectrum of ideas and concepts and allow you to determine the relevance and suitability for your specific situation.

In short, I've loosely drawn parallels between methods applied by mariners and brand managers alike to illustrate both the evolution of and current tactics employed by their practitioners. With twenty-first century technology upon us, a ship's captain or brand manager can utilize a myriad of tools to help plot a course for success. The outcome can be both a safe and timely voyage and the continued health and prosperity of a firm's brand.

Contents

Introduction

Organizations of all kinds forge their brand's strategic trajectory on a daily basis, whether intentionally or unintentionally. This occurs through deliberate planning and execution, chastening of market fads, or response to a competitive threat. Whatever the root cause, a direction emerges, and the consequences unveil themselves somewhere along the brand's journey. Just as a mariner plots his course by virtue of a compass and celestial landmarks, so too does management make use of tools and metrics by which strategic brand goals are achieved.

The essence of branding has two distinct features: it's in constant motion and it is multi-dimensional. With respect to motion, every brand emerges from obscurity and builds momentum year upon year. Over time, the brand develops a personality and becomes a moniker consumers can trust to deliver a certain kind of value. Depending on the business landscape and how the brand has been nurtured, these two features merge and a trajectory crystallizes.

Creation of the Brand Triad

The purpose of creating the brand triad model was three-fold: to develop a visual tool for mapping a brand's current state, to clarify how the brand will solve the customer's problem, and to plot the future direction to create or redefine the brand strategy. In addition, this book was primarily directed toward small to medium-sized companies that typically do not possess the time or budget to invest in this activity.

The road that led me to developing this work was indeed a long one. During my college years, I learned the basics of marketing principles and how advertising was narrowing from mass communication to specialty niches. It wasn't until graduate school that I was introduced to the in-depth study of branding and its growing importance to organizations in a global economy. This awakening drove me to research and read nearly all contributors to this topic. As a result, I predicated my graduate thesis on the subject of branding methodologies: process of branding. My curiosity didn't end there.

My thirst for the examination of branding and strategy drove me to continue my post graduate education via Barnes & Noble. Racking up thousands of dollars over the years, my book shelves are now overflowing! Consuming what industry experts and academia espoused on the topic helped me to monitor this ever changing landscape. The most recent shift, called peer production and content creation, clearly indicates that the brand resides squarely in the hands of consumers. This very idea would have shocked my university professors to their very core.

At the urging of one professor, she suggested I write a spin-off article from my thesis and submit it to both online and offline marketing forums. To date, I've written and published sixteen articles on various aspects of branding and marketing strategy. Years later, I consolidated what I learned and practiced into my first book, *The Brand Advocate: A Strategy-Driven Workbook*. This work was primarily created to introduce small to medium sized firms to basic branding principals in a workbook format. The *Brand Triad*, on the other hand, was developed as a toolbox to analyze the current business state and help uncover possible future directions a firm may choose to take.

Chapter One

A reasonable starting point begins with chapter one and begs the question what is a brand? The content not only defines what a brand is, but also it considers a variety of theories and viewpoints from noted authors. It begins with a brand legacy, or point of origin, to assess how a brand is perceived today based on that lineage. Next we consider what a brand strategy is and what it is not. We also consider how patrons make choices based on their brand loyalty. Finally, we take a look at the client relationship by examining what a nano brand is and how this depth can be achieved.

Chapter Two

Chapter two shifts from brand definition to the fundamentals of the brand triad. This model helps the marketing practitioner or business leader plot the current state of their brand in relation to three key constituents: attributes, behavior, and circumstances. This business tool helps visualize where the brand resides today and what direction, or trajectory, it needs to move in the future. Without this brand assessment, organizations will continue on the path they set long ago. By applying the brand triad, a new trajectory can be set along with providing the process for future evaluations. In addition to brand management issues, other theories of strategic planning and execution will be considered to aid in the assessment of corporate decision making.

Chapter Three

A hypothetical, yet real-world application of the brand triad will be discussed in chapter three. We place the reader in the seat of an executive's role and present current issues facing the airline industry. Armed with the brand triad model, we assess the situation by decoupling the three facets—attributes, behavior, and circumstances—and analyzing each independently. The outcome reveals gaps in the offering (value gap analysis) and defines a new position. These findings then become the actionable items which drive a future brand strategy.

Chapter Four

This final chapter draws together all the elements discovered and discussed in the book. By summarizing the findings, the reader is equipped to practice and apply this toolbox to their specific challenge. Most small to medium sized firms do not possess the tools required to make these evaluations. The brand triad model provides the fundamental building blocks to undertake a much-needed assessment and possible repositioning.

Chapter 1

What is a Brand

Brands have been vital to the promotion and selling of products throughout history. The term brand has come to signify the source or ownership of a product/service and was typically used to mark livestock and other possessions. In commercial terms, a brand is a name, symbol, or other mark that distinguishes goods or services of one group of sellers from another (Hanby, 1999). The more formal practice of branding occurred during America's post-war period and focused on the management of the four Ps: product, price, place, and promotion.

During post-war decades, pent-up demand and a thriving economy encouraged the practice of product management and mass media delivered messages. In an instant, the fundamentals of business changed forever. The 1960s saw the emergence of low-cost, foreign competitors (primarily Japan) followed by globalization of markets in the 1970s. The rise of quality and price competition increased in the 1980s, which led to cost cutting, reengineering, and digitalization of information technology in the 1990s. As a result of price competition and cost reduction, the only sustaining value that remained was a genuine brand.

Genuine Brand

A genuine brand contains three distinct attributes: an internalized sum of impressions, a distinct position in the mind's eye, and a perceived functional and emotional benefit (Knapp, 2000). Knapp contends that brands can be well known but still not distinctive in the customer's mind. The primary objective of genuine brands should be to add value to people's lives. A genuine brand is about benefiting the customer, and the more differentiated a brand is, the easier it is to communicate efficiently with the customer.

Brand Theories: Historic Perspective

Branding has developed over the centuries, and its evolution carries with it a variety of meanings. If we start with academia, Princeton University defines branding as "Trade name: a name given to a product or service." *Merriam-Webster* denotes a brand as "4a: a class of goods identified by name as the product of a single firm or manufacturer: b: a characteristic or distinctive kind." The sheer number of definitions is vast, but I gather you have the idea. Let's now turn to those who have shaped the foundations of branding.

Founding Fathers of Branding

The name Rosser Reeves might sound familiar to those who have studied advertising or have been associated with marketing in one form or another. In his first book, *Reality of Advertising*, Reeves developed the concept of a unique selling proposition (USP). He expresses the concept as something your competitors cannot or will not offer. This 1961 theory remains the basis of many branding concepts, although fashioned and labeled by a variety of authors.

In addition to the AMAs definition of a brand, Philip Kotler suggests that brands "can covey up to six levels of meaning: attributes, benefits, values, culture, personality, and user." Consumer visualization of these six levels on a deeper, more meaningful level is the objective of the professional marketer. He concludes this thought by suggesting a brand's essence is defined by values, culture, and personality.

David Aaker (2004), a noted author in this field, asserts that branding increases credibility and memory, helps communication, and provides the basis for a sustainable, competitive advantage. He also points out that managing the brand requires senior management support and is an organizational issue. Through the years, Aaker has written a substantial volume of work on building brands, and in his latest endeavor he focuses on the concept of a brand portfolio. He emphasizes that the objectives of a brand portfolio are to "foster synergy, leverage brand assets, create and maintain market relevance, build and support differentiated and energized brands, and achieve clarity."

According to Schultz and Barnes (1999), the subject of brands became a hot topic in marketing circles as well as the general business world during the 1980s. They go on to say that interest stemmed from two divergent factors: brand devaluation, due to price competition and an overcrowding of products in the marketplace, and brand acquisition by corporate raiders.

Barnes and Schultz introduced a process called integrated brand communications (IBC). They state that one of the most important concepts of IBC is to consider the financial investment in brand communications (107). They illustrate this idea through a spreadsheet format to demonstrate return on customer investment (ROCI). With ROCI in hand, management can assess the financial implications of investments made and track the results. If the current approach delivers poor results, marketing practitioners can and should continue to readjust their strategy until the right combination of venues achieves the desired outcome (top-line revenue).

A team that has collaborated for twenty-six years, Al Ries and Jack Trout, brought forth to the business world the concept of "positioning." Together they developed *22 Immutable Laws of Marketing*, which set specific laws that companies tend to violate.

Their first law, or the Law of Leadership, seemingly flows through to laws two and three. Regarding the Law of Leadership, Ries and Trout suggest it's better to be first than to be better—perceptions not products. Citing the first person to cross the Atlantic in a plane—Charles Lindbergh—they pose the question, "who was second?" They follow with the Law of Category, which implies that if you can't be the first in one category then find another one: Amelia Earhart was the first woman to cross the Atlantic. Their third law, the law of the mind, states it's better to be first in the mind than in the marketplace. Taken together, these axioms define the central message Ries and Trout have touted beyond simple marketing approaches—positioning. In my opinion, they help define a business strategy.

Scott Davis advocates that brands are one of a firm's most valuable assets, and leveraging them can help achieve profitable growth initiatives. Davis characterizes a brand as a relationship that involves trust, consistency, a defined set of expectations, and existence in the customer's mind. As noted in his book, *Brand Asset Management*, Davis developed a framework that consists of four phases and eleven steps. His methodology starts with developing a brand vision and follows with crafting a brand picture. The heart of his process follows in the next five steps, which revolve around a brand management strategy. The final two steps in phase four measure both the culture and return on investment. Taken together, Davis suggests brands are assets that should be managed on the basis of financial return and growth.

In his introduction to *A New Brand World*, Scott Bedbury, whose credentials include the crafting and nurturing of Nike and Starbucks brands, insists that "supporting and building a brand is everyone's job." He continues by stating "Building a brand is the most challenging, complicated, and painstaking process that a company can embark on." In his book, Bedbury provides eight principles for achieving brand leadership.

These principles include defining and protecting your brand's DNA and making your brand's values pervasive in your organization. With respect to DNA, Bedbury suggests that cracking the genetic code is not about a product but an essence and ethos that define your organization/brand . Regarding a parenting role, Bedbury espouses someone in the organization should be accountable for the brand, such as a chief brand officer, to assure both business and brand goals are aligned.

My final historic perspective was derived from Douglas Holt's recent book, *How Brands Become Icons*. In chapter one, Holt suggests that cultural icons are pervasive in our society and can be both human and nonhuman. He goes on to say that people strongly relate to and use these icons in their daily lives, and, in some cases, icons provide the basis of meaning.

The locus of Holt's work implies that iconic brands address the desires and anxieties of a culture during a turbulent period in history. A good example was Coke's 1971 commercial "teach the world to sing" that spoke of unity during the Vietnam conflict. These identity myths are embedded in the product, and we experience them through its usage . He also insinuates that myths are set in populist worlds and are performed by activists who lead cultural change. Finally, Holt distinguishes cultural branding from conventional models—mind share, emotional, and viral branding techniques—and uses case studies to demonstrate its value.

Brand Theory Summation

As you can see, scholars and business consultants have theorized and pontificated on the many facets of branding. Although it may appear these ideologies compete or are in conflict with each other, I view it differently. Over the past fifteen years, I've digested the majority of books and articles on this subject and now recognize the similarities, patterns, and truisms. In some cases, the underpinnings and precepts only differ in approach and terminology. In the world of brand gurus, we can all contribute to and build on the current base of knowledge to the benefit of those we serve—marketing practitioners.

BRAND EVALUATIONS AND OUTCOMES

Now that we have a general understanding of branding, what's our next step? As with any venture, a situational analysis helps your organization take inventory of the business, environment, and changes in the marketplace. It's no different with your brand model. Kotler and Armstrong (1991) suggest this type of examination will determine problem areas and opportunities, and it will recommend a plan of action to improve the company's marketing performance. An analysis involves the current state of aesthetics or identity and entails discovering what the offering represents in order to uncover corporate or customer impressions (Schmitt, 1997).

A *Harvard Business Review* article proposed that brand positioning starts with establishing a frame of reference, which signals to consumers the goal they can expect to achieve by using the brand (Keller, 2002). This theory suggests that all businesses are required to understand the frame of reference in which their brands operate and to compare points of difference and points of parity with those of their competitors.

Rosser Reeves advocates the use of a unique selling proposition (USP) for each brand and the consistent promotion of that message

(Kotler, 1997). Barnes and Schultz (1999) insist that, when conducting a brand business review, any attempt to develop a program is generally unsuccessful without fully understanding the brand, its customers, and the marketplace.

Brand Assessment

Evaluating your brand and determining what outcomes you are seeking should be the first order of business. Many small to medium sized firms are so focused on sales growth (as they should be) that the brand model has been left unattended. The identity of any organization develops over time and becomes a by-product of legacy engagements. In effect, the culmination of past business accounts, markets, and perceptions become the organization's new reality! Don't believe me?

Pick any business in any industry and take a moment to determine your impression of that firm. Your perception has little to do with today's reality. Any product or service we purchase or use has a history (legacy), and as consumers we rely on the consistency of those prior experiences to reduce hesitation, anxiety, or pain. In fact, we trust that these legacy promises will continue into the future.

As a result, forging your brand reputation from the start will pay dividends into the future. This point doesn't discount the fact that firms grow, evolve, and reinvigorate over time. What it does suggest— managing your brand development, growth, and repositioning over time—should be as important as top-line sales growth.

Now that we have considered branding from both a historic and an assessment point-of-view, let's turn to the many facets of branding. These include brand legacy, strategy, loyalty, and something new called nano branding. These tools will help the brand practitioner assess the brand's lineage, direction, compelling allure, and depth to which consumers truly know and associate with it. Taken together, chapter one will form the basis of brand usefulness.

Brand Legacy

My neighbor owned a local Italian restaurant; they served authentic food and were especially well known for their mouthwatering pizzas. Each night of the week they were busy with people standing in line for a table. Their brand legacy was a combination of Mama's old fashioned recipes (she was from Sicily) and the restaurant's interior design, which resembled a comfortable Italian home. Soon Roundtable, Domino's, and an assortment of pizza firms inundated the local area and offered speed of service over authenticity. Feeling the pressure of competition, Mama's strayed from her winning brand proposition (traditional Italian food) to mimic the competition. Today, the once time-honored cuisine and Sicilian ambiance (experience) has been replaced with cookie-cutter pizzas, video games, and a service counter. Any remnant of Mama's legacy has disappeared and, with it, a differentiated brand.

What exactly is a brand legacy? I searched the American Marketing Association's "Dictionary of Marketing Terms" (marketingpower.com), Google, and Yahoo and found no such official term. As a result, I've coined the term and have provided a definition that suggests that the foundations of your brand can have an impact on your current brand strategy.

Brand Legacy Defined

A brand legacy is your targeted audience's current perception of your product or service. It begins from a point of origin (core idea) and considers historic message layering.

All brands possess a starting point (like a cornerstone of a building), and each additional "brick" adds to the ultimate shape of the "building." Think back to 1984: Apple produced a commercial that ran only once, in which a female runner sped through a crowd of clones to launch a hammer at the screen of "Big Brother." The message from Apple—we're different!

Apple's many innovations both support and validate the initial core idea made in 1984. These include application icons on a desktop (versus MSDOS prompts), multi-colored desktop computers, the first commercially available mouse, and innovative software applications (Quick Time). Despite a few bumps in the road (Newton, for example), Apple has stayed true to their brand legacy. Recent product offerings such as the iPod (Mini, Shuffle, and Nano; iPhone; iTouch) reinforce this core idea to their constituency.

Another example of a brand legacy can be provided by asking you to ponder Volkswagen (VW). The origin of VW was the Beetle brand, which spoke to a specific audience (the people's car). Although VW pursued a myriad of vehicle designs and brand offerings (the Thing, Passat, Cabrio, Golf, Jetta, etc.), since its introduction in the 1950s, the number of new car sales in North America shrank from a half-million cars to only forty thousand units by 1990. When VW decided to resurrect the Beetle, sales skyrocketed. The Beetle reintroduction helped bolster sales increases in all other models, and VW produced four hundred twenty-five thousand units by the turn of the century. In this case, the legacy (Beetle) not only enhanced the VW brand, in many ways, it was the brand.

Brand Legacy Example

During a recent speaking engagement, I wanted to demonstrate to the audience the power of a brand legacy. My visual presentation displayed the United Airlines (UAL) logo on screen, and I asked the audience to tell me the company's byline (sometimes referred to as a tagline). Most hands shot high in the air, and one participant yelled out "Fly the friendly skies." I alluded that UAL had made a change(s) and asked for the current theme. The room fell silent. I then displayed the 1997 byline "Rising" and the 2004 "It's Time to Fly" campaign. As with this audience, the flying public in general has a right to be confused: during a recent flight on UAL, the safety video played the familiar *Rhapsody in Blue* piano piece (auditory reminder of the past) and even used the original slogan at the end of the video. Is it the "Friendly Skies" or "Time to Fly"? I'm not sure.

UAL once served (legacy) as a moniker for an elegant, professional, and friendly airline. As a 100K, or one hundred thousand mileage flier, I was so enamored by their service and offerings in the early 1990s that I only flew UAL and was extremely brand loyal. By 1997, they tried to enhance the business traveler's mindset regarding customer service through a new byline titled "Rising." Next, they introduced United Express (aimed at discount travel) on many routes, and my fierce devotion began to wane. Since then, they've again changed their byline to "Time to Fly," cut services, rolled out an airline within an airline called "Ted," and reduced the mileage program benefits. At this point, they are following the same path that Mama took with her Italian eatery.

With the Brand Legacy definition and a few examples in hand, let's return to the original question posed—what is the next move as it pertains to *your* brand legacy? To plan these moves, we need to start with your core idea. From there, we can begin to map a future direction.

Core Idea

As mentioned in the brand legacy definition, the final summation a consumer (whether B2B or B2C) extracts from your brand is a core idea. A core idea is a word or thought that encompasses all facets of your brand. Let's try a few: Hershey's = chocolate; Quaker Oats = oatmeal; Chevron = gasoline; IBM = computers; Macy's = department store; Hollywood = movies.

We practice the use of these core ideas every day to aid us with our consumption habits. If we are hungry, we mentally sort through all the brands available and select one that closely resembles an ideal core brand. Every time you make a choice, there resides a point of reference or origin from which you base your purchasing criteria.

A noted Harvard Professor and author, Dr. Clayton Christenson (2003), phrased it another way: "the functional, emotional, and social dimensions of the jobs that customers need to get done constitute the circumstances in which they buy."

Let's expand upon this core idea concept to understand the dimensions of choice. A core idea operates on three distinct levels. The brand radar depicted below may be used to visually demonstrate these differences.

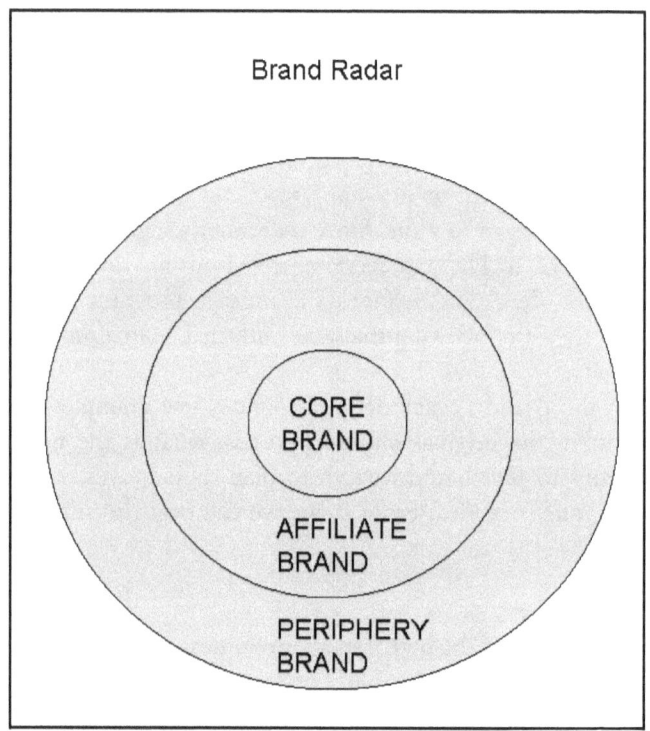

Core Brand

This represents the true or original core idea. The constituents of the core possess something that cannot be substituted.

Affiliate Brand

Although closely associated with the core idea, this surrounding area represents a close approximation or facsimile.

Periphery Brand

This represents a distant offering that maintains some resemblance to the original core idea.

We can apply these three levels by viewing, for example, the habits of devout coffee drinkers. First, we need to narrow the target audience down to those consumers who buy-on-the-run versus those who make their own coffee. The habits of our mobile consumers can be observed at any coffeehouse. Their profile resembles the following: always rushing, always having something specific in mind, and always demanding consistency and quality. Whether walk-in or drive-through, these people don't have time to relax and enjoy the ambiance of the coffeehouse.

For this particular target audience, they have a set pattern or behavior. In their minds, only the core brand will suffice. I happen to be one of those mobile people. I see the same faces at Starbucks each morning, at the same time, ordering roughly the same products. I took the opportunity to ask different patrons why they stopped there each morning. The resounding response was "I love Starbucks coffee!" When I suggested Dietrich's, an affiliate brand down the street, the variety of contorted looks ranged from confusion to "you're crazy." I'm sure if I visited with the Dietrich's crowd, I would garner the same response towards Starbucks. The point here is that we strive for the original whenever possible. As a brand manager, this type of response is exactly what you want out of your patrons.

Imagine the following scenario: you're traveling in another city, and the concierge at your hotel hasn't the faintest clue where to find a Starbucks. Although your profile remains the same—mobile consumer—you instinctively broaden your brand acceptability to those products or services that are adjacent to the core. An affiliate brand for the mobile consumer could include other coffeehouses that share the same attributes as the original. Depending on the city, this subset may include Dietrich's, Seattle's Best, Caribou, or any facsimile of the original. I was in Minneapolis recently and confronted with the same dilemma. Fortunately, my friend directed me to the nearest Caribou Coffee, where the aesthetics are very similar: design, ambiance, taste; and my expectations were met (to a degree).

Although you have the idea by now, the periphery brand has the lowest ranking, and these brands are purchased in the absence of no other choice. These offerings include doughnut shops, mom and pop stores, and the mart area at gas stations. Believe it or not, all of these venues promote their periphery brands, which are derived from the core brand. Are you not convinced? Look at the display signs and designs—colors, visual images—used on the foam cups and the similar brand names they use. They all, in one way or another, resemble the core idea.

AN ORGANIZATION'S BRAND LEGACY

When I was a child, we used to play on a hill that was carved away by a bulldozer. The bulldozer uncovered layers of strata, or sedimentary layers, that had accumulated over thousands of years. As we dug through this hillside, it was apparent that the topsoil looked very different from what was beneath. The same can be said for many companies (brands) today.

Let's consider McDonalds. The core idea of this fast-food restaurant was hamburgers, fries, and shakes at affordable prices and quick service. The first facility was built in 1940 and grew as a franchise business. By 1957, a motto was created that permeated throughout the nearly one hundred stores: Quality, Service, Cleanliness and Value (Q.S.C. & V.). As history records it, it's safe to say the core idea was: McDonalds = Hamburgers.

Fast-forward to 2008. After many decades of advertising layering, promotions, slogans, and jingles, what does McDonalds equal today? It certainly is unclear. Over the years, they've introduced breakfast items, ribs and steak sandwiches, burgers for grown-ups, healthy meals (a variety of salads), and specialty desserts. Just like the sedimentary hillside we used to play on, I know somewhere in those layers of messaging still resides a basic hamburger. Have they drifted too far from the core idea?

Have you heard of In-n-Out Burgers? If you ever visit California, Nevada, or Arizona, you'll likely find one just off the freeway. What is their brand legacy? Hamburgers! Even their jingle stays true to the core: *"In-n-Out, In-n-Out, that's what a hamburger is all about!"* No confusion here.

Let's Focus on Your Brand

What about your brand legacy? Let's start with your point of origin. If someone asked ten people in your organization to answer the following equation, would the answers be the same?

Your company's core idea = _____

How did the answers stack up? Were they similar or vastly different? No matter what business you are in, you should be remembered for one thing or idea. The next obvious question should be what business are you in today? If your past (point of origin) and present (perception) do not match, then its time to reexamine your brand legacy and analyze what it means.

Depending on the landscape of your industry or business, you have one of three strategic choices for your brand legacy:

1) Embrace

2) Discard

3) Reinvent

Embrace

Let's look at a few organizations that have embraced their brand legacy. Both VWs Beetle and Ford's Mustang have returned to their roots and leveraged the heritage of their core idea. In effect, they took the original car concept and modernized the design to include conveniences and amenities that the buying public would demand today. The brand legacies instilled in the Beetle and Mustang are more than just names or symbols; they represent a legend or storyline that consumers can follow. Because the shell, or chassis, resembles the original, this visual perception was enough to prompt a purchase. According to Chris Zook, in his book *Profit from the Core*, "Companies that have very few, highly focused, core businesses account for most of the sustained growth companies." He continues by stating "companies that sustained at least a 5.5 annual growth over ten years shows that 80% of these value creators had one core business with clear market leadership."

Discard

In 1984, Integrated Electronics Co. (later known as Intel) produced dynamic random access memory chips, or DRAM, by the millions, and this was their main source of income. The onslaught of Japanese companies—Fujitsu, Hitachi, NEC, and Toshiba—invaded this market space and proved to be more efficient with 80 percent to 90 percent yield rates compared to Intel's success rate of 50 percent to 80 percent. By the mid-eighties, Intel was losing market share due to low prices and the dumping of chips into North America. Andy Grove, Intel's CEO, made a tough decision: discard the manufacturing of DRAM chips and focus all of their energy and efforts on the development of microprocessors. In 1989, following Moore's Law of doubling power and halving costs every eighteen months, Intel transformed itself from a marginally profitable commodity memory chip maker into the producer of the standard processor that drove all the world's computers. The 1990 "Intel Inside" campaign, in effect, solidified their new core brand position.

Reinvent

What comes to mind when you think of baking soda? Would you agree that most consumers would respond with Arm & Hammer?

In 1846, Dr. Austin Church and John Dwight set out to sell sodium bicarbonate in little boxes. By 1867, Dr. Church retired, and his two sons formed Church & Co. and introduced the hammer wielding arm of Vulcan (the god of fire) to their packages. Through the years, this simple product found new applications including cooking, personal care, household agent, deodorizer, laundry detergent, and dental care. The Arm & Hammer web site succinctly states their value proposition:

ARM & HAMMER Baking Soda—pure, versatile, effective, environmentally safe, and economical. Evidence that good solutions for your home, your family, and your body are timeless.

As with Arm & Hammer, it doesn't mean that you abandon your core, you merely find new ways to leverage your brand legacy.

Your Next Move

We defined your brand legacy and filtered out the core idea. Next, we evaluated what your core brand represents and identified the affiliate and periphery brands that surround your market space. Finally, we charted a course for your brand (embrace, discard, reinvent). The next step is to integrate this brand strategy into your future marketing plans.

A word of caution: great care must be considered when you take this next step. For Andy Grove, it was huge: he laid off three thousand workers, sought government protectionism against foreign competition, and walked away from his base business. His calculated moves were made to save Intel.

When Michael Eisner was considering the CEO position at Walt Disney in 1984, the company was stumbling along and vultures loomed overhead. Eisner embraced the Disney legacy and put into play the many assets the organization had locked away in a vault. He, in effect, generated cash by raising theme park fees, releasing the classics to video, purchasing ABC, and investing heavily into new films and entertainment venues. By embracing the Mouse, Eisner generated $65 billion in market wealth for this organization.

Another bold business leader—Jack Welch—laid off nearly one hundred thousand workers in 1981 and radically restructured the composition of the company he was hired to reinvent. His mantra was be first or second in the marketplace or get out! Although his approach seemed unconventional, he did convert GE into one of the most valued corporations in the world.

Your next move may not be as earth-shattering as Grove, Eisner, or Welch, but in your organization it may be the next plausible direction your company will take. After careful analysis, you may discern that your organization is not growing, hardly profitable, or just stagnant in your designated market space. As Chris Zook suggested in his book, *Profit from the Core*, narrowing your focus and strengthening your core values will drive top and bottom-line results. Zook goes on to suggest that only after you have a strong core do you venture out to an adjacent business as a growth strategy.

Summation

We began our discussion with a definition of brand legacy and a suggestion that your core idea or point of origin can impact your current perception. Often what customers remember through years of message layering creates confusion if the message conflicts with today's meaning. We also explored three aspects of the core idea by breaking them down into three constituents: core, affiliate, and periphery brands. Your position on the brand radar as it pertains to the competition remains the key to your future trajectory.

Next, we considered your brand legacy and what your core idea equates to today. We also presented three possible strategies for your organization to consider: embrace, discard, or reinvent your brand. Several examples demonstrated how business leaders took bold actions to change their strategic direction. The challenge for your brand legacy remains—what is your next move?

Brand Strategy

What constitutes a brand strategy? I've often seen organizations undertake a branding process, yet the net outcome closely resembles a public relations face-lift. Why does this occur? One possibility might be the framework that guides the process. Another may simply be the viewpoint of the agency or consultant employed. In any case, valuable dollars are spent each year on brand strategy endeavors, and frequently the outcome does not yield the tangible results organizations are seeking.

What is a Brand Strategy?

Let's begin our discovery process by seeking an understanding and interpretation from experts in the field of branding. In *Building Strong Brands,* David Aaker implies the "objective of a brand strategy ... is to create a business that resonates with customers." Aaker also suggests this process must involve an analysis from three perspectives: customer, competitor, and self analysis. Another expert, David Arnold (1992), suggests a "brand strategy is the process whereby the offer is positioned in the customer's mind to produce a perception of advantage."

By its very essence, a strategy implies the execution of the organization's vision, mission, and overarching objectives. The same should hold true for a brand strategy: a series of steps or methodologies, which explain the brand development and execution. In my experience, some organizations bypass this critical juncture intentionally or unknowingly.

Now that we have defined what constitutes a brand strategy, let's understand how your organization develops a strategy. Does it follow a methodology that demands self-reflection of your process or an artistic rendition that capitalizes on imagery rather than business acumen? If the latter sentence strikes a cord with you, whether positively or otherwise, then the following information just may inspire you to delve deeper into your brand strategy.

Evaluation

When an organization seeks guidance from a branding firm, the strategic intent may be well defined. Usually a consulting firm absorbs all facets of the marketing problem and later returns with a plan to solve a particular situation. The question remains—what process did the consultant utilize to derive their proposed solution? Because we have a natural tendency to rely on the expertise of industry leaders, we tend to forgo the analysis and process that supports the underpinning logic. How many times have we visited the family physician and taken their recommendations with absolute trust? In the same manner, our faith in marketing consultants has risen to new heights. Although the advice we have received may indeed be sound, the application of a method to test this process would be a worthy investment.

Methodology

For over seventeen years, in an effort to stay current on the topic of branding, I've invested in books and business trade journals that were authored by both academia and industry leaders. The litmus test to the many theories I've read about resides in how applicable and relevant they are to real world situations. In some cases, these concepts reinforced the fundamentals that were simply forgotten along the way. Still others explored new dimensions that were groundbreaking and worthy of debate. The challenge remains for your organization—should you invest in your own understanding to better manage the results of a quality brand strategy?

Reference Materials

If you are a newcomer to branding, or simply need to brush up on the topic, understanding the basics will enhance your interaction with the marketing consultant. I would recommend a book by Scott Bedbury called *A New Brand World*. Bedbury talks about branding fundamentals and applies his branding experience at Starbucks and

Nike to demonstrate salience in real world applications. Once the basics are covered, you'll need a method by which to manage and control the process. The temptation to relinquish control of your brand might evolve as your relationship with your consultant deepens, but in the end, you are ultimately responsible for its destiny.

The application of a branding process provides a checklist for developing and sustaining your brand. Another excellent reference for your professional library should include *The Brand Mindset* by Duane Knapp. Knapp instills a methodology that is both intelligent in design and practical in implementation. His circular process demands the active reflection and nurturing of your brand. This template can be applied whether you are employing the services of a branding firm or simply undertaking this effort on your own. Either way, it's a fine road map!

If you are a brand aficionado, you may desire to sharpen your skills by reading *Brand Asset Management* by Scott Davis. Davis presents branding as a valuable asset that can be managed through a disciplined process. His approach begins with a brand vision, constructs a strategy, and concludes by measuring the return on brand investment (ROBI). If every facet of your organization applies metrics to evaluate performance, why not apply the same process to a method that governs your most valuable asset?

Analysis

We would all agree the business world moves at breakneck speeds and our ability to harness tools to make successful decisions are scarce. Unless we continually invest in our professional marketing discipline, the ability to discern what process we should follow and the expected ROBI will flounder.

Conclusion

In his recent book, *Seeing What's Next*, Dr. Christensen noted that companies are valued by three rigors: resources, process, and values. Because most organizations can acquire resources, it's the application of your process (how you solve problems) and values (past investments) that determine success. If this concept rings true to you, then the methodology you employ in branding (process) and your values (investments) will ultimately determine your future success!

Brand Loyalty

What drives brand loyalty? The psychology behind human behavior as it pertains to brand selection can be both rudimentary and complicated at the same time. We will explore this conundrum by investigating noted authors' insights into the realm of brand preference. By unveiling current research and opinions of experts, a convergence of ideologies will advocate techniques in order to deepen current and potential relationships. Methods will be introduced which evoke the use of our five senses to evaluate, develop, and drive a deeply-rooted brand preference. Let's begin by understanding how we interact with our surroundings.

Communications Model

To better understand the process of preference, let's first look at a basic communications model. The five components of this model are sender, medium, filter, receiver, and feedback. On a daily basis we are exposed to messages (sender/medium) via radio, television, billboards, Internet, mail, and word-of-mouth. All messages are coded patterns and sensations—colors, sounds, odors, shapes. Although these messages are pervasive, we continually screen out or ignore content that has little or no relevance to us. The messages we deem recognizable, or the basis for a relationship, are decoded and stored in our memory (filter/screen). A successful convergence between sender and receiver will result in some type of response to a brand's compelling message (feedback).

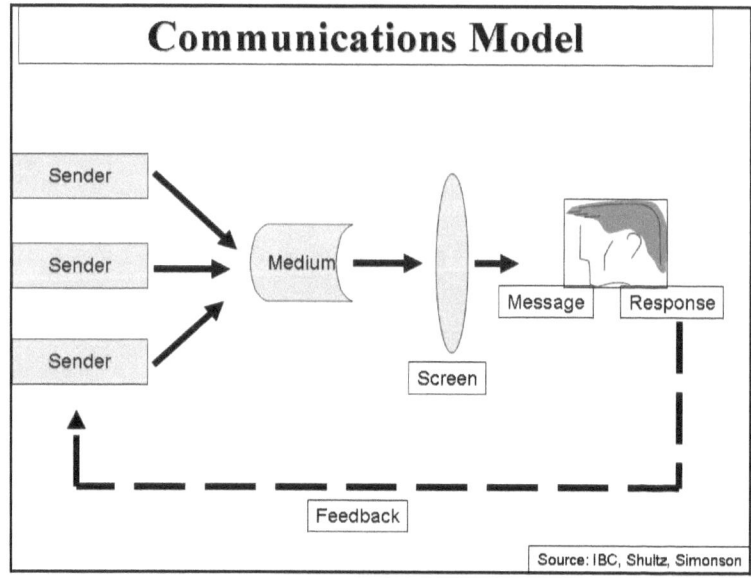

Stored experiences in our long-term memory are connected through a series of nodes and networks. An example could be all of the associations you might have with the word Starbucks including coffee, rich aroma, relaxing, sofa, and earth tones. As presented by Schultz and Barnes in *Strategic Brand Communications Campaigns* (1999), "this node and connection process, called spreading activation, makes every person different." Because we all have different experiences, connections, and relationships, this supports a theory that the *consumer*, not the organization, owns the brand.

Brand Loyalty Defined

So, what constitutes brand loyalty? According to Bloemer and Kasper, brand loyalty implies that consumers bind themselves to products or services as a result of a deep-seated commitment. To exemplify this point, they rendered a distinction between repeat purchases and actual brand loyalty. In their published research, they assert that a repeat purchase behavior "is the actual re-buying of a brand;" whereas, loyalty includes "antecedents," or reasons or facts occurring before the behavior.

Bloemer and Kasper further delineate brand loyalty into "spurious" and "true" loyalty. "Spurious and true loyalty are both biased, behavioral responses expressed over time by some decision making unit, with respect to one or more alternate brands. However, spurious loyalty is a function of inertia, that is to say the consumer is more likely than not to stick with one product because it is easier than changing to another product. True brand loyalty, on the other hand, is not a function of inertia but a psychological process that results in brand commitment."

Ref: Journal of Economic Psychology, Volume 16, Issue 2, July 1995.) Let's now turn to how this psychology plays out in the branding process.

Brand Positioning

Organizations seek to develop and project brand perceptions based on internally driven needs and goals rather than seek input from their targeted audience. In Jack Trout's book, *Differentiate or Die*, he presents and defends his theories on consumer behavior and interpretation as they relate to brand perception. Although these concepts seem self-evident on the surface, organizations tend to ignore these immutable laws in their daily branding activities.

Human Inability to Assimilate Information

Due to the sheer volume of messages we encounter on a daily basis, the human mind can't begin to cope with interpreting them all. Trout notes some statistics on how our minds can't cope, are limited, and are insecure:

- Humans tolerate constant daily electronic bombardment
- Four thousand books are published around the world every day
- The world wide web grows by one million pages each day

Our Minds are Limited

- Perceptions are selective
- Memory is highly selective
- Physiological limitations inhibit the processing of stimuli

Our Minds are Insecure

- Mind's are both emotional and rational
- Minds remember things that no longer exist—recall

What conclusions can we draw from these statistics? As previously mentioned, I asked an audience if they knew the current tagline for United Airlines. They resoundingly responded with "Fly the friendly skies!" When I pointed out that United changed its tag in 1997 to "Rising" and again in 2004 to "Its Time to Fly," they were astonished. Despite the millions of dollars United spent on this ad campaign (minds can't cope and are limited), the audience only recalled something that didn't exist (minds are insecure). When drafting your brand positioning strategy, you may want to consider your previous message layering activities and determine if your new value proposition enhances or conflicts in the minds of your intended audience. You may recall, a value proposition is a unique value a business offers to its customers. Let's examine a technique to analyze brand perceptions.

Brand Molecule

A brand molecule, according to Hill and Lederer, is the process of identifying all associations connected to your brand (2000). In addition to understanding the type of connections, you will need to evaluate the importance of each association and how much weight it carries independently.

By unfolding a brand molecule, the organization is able to view all possible connections, either positive or negative, in its current state. By virtue of this analysis, you can achieve greater clarity and insight into your positioning or rebranding process.

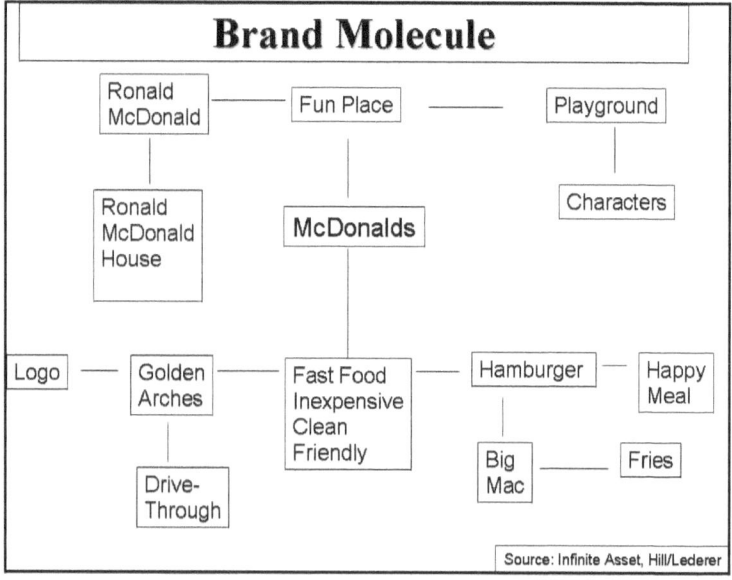

The McDonalds brand molecule, as portrayed in this pictorial, illuminates the basic constructs of this process. Key elements of this model include: linking all brand associations (emanating from the center), the importance of each (size), and how they relate to each other. Once accomplished, you can begin the process of removing those associations that no longer fit and adding new relevant identifiers in their place. This process provides the manager an opportunity to view the entire brand and affect change in a strategic manner.

An example of this process was the recent transformation of Cadillac. In the late 80s and early 90s, sales for this brand were declining due to European and Japanese penetration into the luxury car market. To reverse this erosion, the Cadillac group invested in the brand molecule analysis to reinvent both the design and market preference. This brand was meticulously assessed, disassembled, reassembled, and repositioned in the late 1990s from something grandpa drove into a fast, sexy, and desirable product. Today, you know a Caddy commercial is playing when you hear Led Zeppelin's "Rock and Roll" blaring through the speakers.

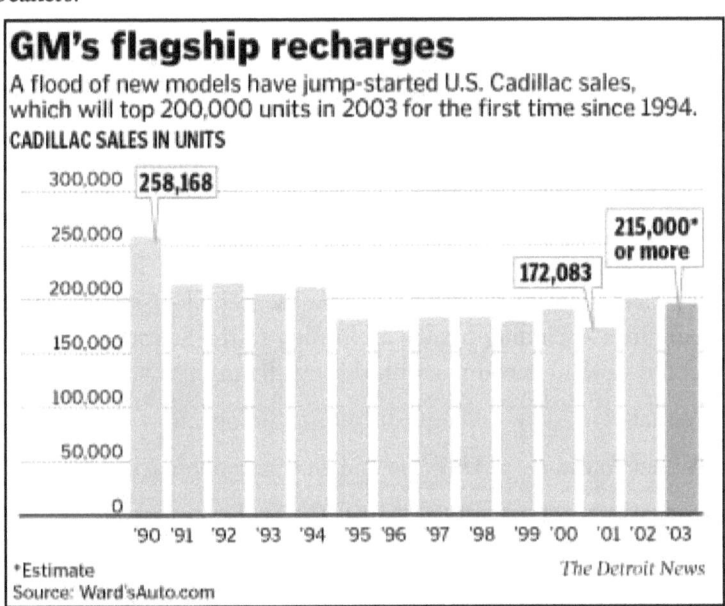

GM's flagship recharges

A flood of new models have jump-started U.S. Cadillac sales, which will top 200,000 units in 2003 for the first time since 1994.

CADILLAC SALES IN UNITS

258,168

215,000* or more

172,083

'90 '91 '92 '93 '94 '95 '96 '97 '98 '99 '00 '01 '02 '03

*Estimate
Source: Ward'sAuto.com

The Detroit News

Sensory Approach

The most innovative brand research I've encountered recently was derived from Martin Lindstrom and his *Brand Sense* concept. A precursor to his theory lies in three components of sensory branding:

- Stimulating your relationship with the brand
- Allowing emotional response to dominate rational thinking
- Differentiating between dimensions of a single brand

When combined, these components build loyalty, emotional engagement, and what Lindstrom terms smashability.

The essence of Lindstrom's work lies in what he terms the Six Sensory Steps. These include (1) Sensory Audit, (2) Brand Staging, (3) Brand Drama, (4) Brand Signature, (5) Implementation, and (6) Evaluation. Through this discovery method, an organization can unveil aspects of their current offering or new avenues to exploit. This process, according to the author, will enhance brand loyalty and deepen existing relationships.

Because we can't possibly delve into all six steps, a cursory view of a few elements of this process is provided. Lindstrom's approach to brand loyalty stems from the use of our five senses. In order to understand any brand, a sensory audit must be conducted to assess the brand's leveraging of sensory touch points. This is comprised of examining a brand's stimuli, enhancement, and bonding capabilities. Lindstrom's point is simply the more sensory components, the stronger the foundation of your brand.

Another area discussed is the synergy across sensory touch points. Lindstrom suggests we use many senses when evaluating our surroundings, including brands. Returning to the Starbucks example, one could view an encounter with this retailer in this manner:

Visual   Unique logo on building, cups, and bags

Visual/Auditory   Uniform and customer approach

Visual/Auditory/Touch   Interior aesthetics (sofa, colors, wall paper, music)

Smell/Taste Distinct aroma released of freshly ground coffee

When analyzing your brand, how strong are the links between each of your sensory touch points? How interdependent are they? In the beginning of this article we mentioned Lindstrom's term smashability. This simply means how independent is each sensory aspect and what is the ability to stand on its own? If you removed the Starbucks logo from the building, would you still know the brand?

Summation

In order to understand the psychology of brand loyalty, we undertook this journey by examining a basic communications model and the process of receiving/filtering messages. Next we reviewed research that suggested a distinction between spurious and true brand loyalty. Several truisms concerning how a brand is positioned in the marketplace revealed the challenges with marketing to the human mind. Finally, we surveyed research that submits the essence of brands is connected through our five senses. The culmination of this information may help any organization facing brand loyalty issues with their constituents and may provide resources to uncover core issues.

Nano Brands

We've all heard the phrase niche marketing and what that means to narrow the focus of both your communications and business model. Most consumer-based industries have slowly migrated from microsegmentation down to the individual consumer. But is that enough?

The challenge most organization's face is how deep is your relationship with current and potential customers? Not unlike most valued relationships, you must anticipate their wants, behaviors, thought processes, and future needs. These desires are expressed through a variety of sensory activities and will be unveiled in this next section. through a concept I call nano branding.

Nano Branding Defined

What is a nano brand? It simply means moving a brand into the deepest level imaginable within the mind's eye of the client. You achieve this by creating a new value that's not currently available and executing it in such a way that's hard to follow. Starbucks took generic coffee drinkers and, by changing the rules of the game, turned them into committed brand patriots! Serious joggers invest in shoe technology and will only consider the Nike brand to other competing offerings. If you need a package sent overnight and demand assurance it will get there, your only consideration would be Fed-X. In the same respect, understanding the value required in a given setting drives brand commitment. This changes the client's view from casual user to a committed brand owner. Let's apply nano branding to the hotel industry and consider the possibilities.

Application of Nano Branding

To set the stage, we first need to understand the context of this hotel–consumer relationship. At first blush, any current or potential customer would discern hotel brands through a variety of venues: an advertisement, signage, travel agent suggestion, Internet (and Internet portals), recommendation from a colleague, and general word-of-mouth. In some cases, you only have one opportunity to introduce your value proposition, and first impressions are critical. One question remains: how engaging and innovative is this hotel–consumer relationship?

In the twenty-first century, current and potential consumers will most likely utilize a web site to begin their price or availability search. The discount shopper will typically seek third-party sites (hotels.com, Expedia, Priceline, etc.), but highly valued consumers are generally business travelers and prefer a direct connection with a brand. Henceforth, we'll refer to business travelers as clients.

To assure consistency, I viewed five commonly known hotel websites and followed their respective processes from the home page to checkout. The brands included Marriott, Westin, Hyatt, Hilton, and Crowne Plaza. To evaluate each brand, I sought accommodations in a progressive city—Irvine, California—and used each site to secure a reservation.

In each case, all hotel companies offered nearly the same experience. They allowed the client to search city, state, and dates of travel. In addition, they all offered various rates based on type of room and other accommodations. The number of clicks to achieve a valid reservation ranged from three to five web pages.

Let's assume a match occurred between a client and a desired room rate. At this juncture, all hotel brands usher you off to checkout and miss a *huge* opportunity! From the hotel management's point-of-view, their job is done. From the client's experience, it's good enough but no better than any other offering. The following suggests an alternate approach to relationship and brand enhancement.

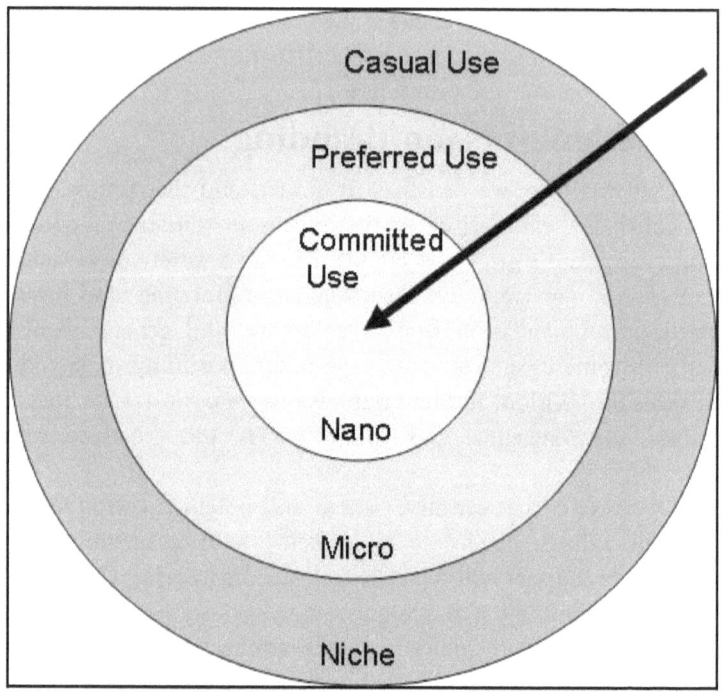

Dare to Dream:

Imagine if clients were treated differently. In addition to selecting criteria such as a nonsmoking room and a king-size bed, consider the unveiling of offerings that would enhance their experience and build brand loyalty at the same time? After a client completes the reservation essentials, gently draw them to a world where they can customize their experience. Using current information technology and infrastructure most hotel companies employ, let's imagine a full-service hotel chain which seeks to change the rules of the game. How could this be done? Let's break the hotel experience into fragments and address each component.

Room Ambience

When a client walks into your hotel room, what is their first impression? Is the room pitch black? Do they fumble to find the light switch? Once the light is turned on, what do they see? Is the room silent and uninviting? If you stayed one night in each of the brands mentioned previously, would the experience differ?

Now imagine a world where valued clients can specify their preferences. Consider a page on your web site that graphically depicts a standard room. A pop-up invites the client to explore this interactive site and the many surprises to be discovered. By highlighting various objects on the web page, the client can now set the tone of the experience from lighting to the genre of music (through the TV, a CD player, or satellite music devices). After each click by your captivated client, the audio and visual elements on the web page change to reflect the expected brand promise: lighting in the room changes and a sample music clip plays. To fully engage your client, you must attend to all of their senses.

One important caveat—ask the client during his or her first visit if they would like to save their settings before checking out. In this manner, the client wins because this hotel took the time to ask *and* remember their preferences, and in turn, the hotel also wins by deepening their relationship and achieving personal desires. This simple interaction will pay enormous dividends in the form of future revenue streams.

Amenities

This particular client has now experienced something new and inviting and returns to your web site to book his or her next visit. After completing the reservation, he or she runs the cursor around the room graphic and comes across a menu perched on the desk. How about a fruit plate or favorite bottled water in addition to the proper room ambience? These amenities can be ordered through this same venue and delivered by room service.

What's happening here? Two distinct and simultaneous events are occurring that generate *real value*. The client is empowered to customize the experience and begin trusting the brand to deliver the kind of relationship that is desired. For the hotel, a deeper relationship has developed in addition to a greater share of wallet. As you can see, this forum moves the client from price to experience offered and from casual to preferred user.

Food and Beverage

As your client—now preferring this type of treatment—becomes more familiar with his or her profile on your web site, he or she begins to seek new venues of gratification. Does your client enjoy a cup of coffee and toast at 6:25a.m. each morning? How about dining facilities—if you have the best shrimp creole in town, ask if they would like a reservation during their stay. If your client enjoys a martini after work, have one waiting for them. You can now visualize the deepening of the brand–client relationship from casual usage to a must have. Can you hear the cash register ringing yet?

Services

Does your client golf or play tennis after work? Do they enjoy the theatre, or are they an avid movie buff? Whatever their pleasure, you need to know these things. Sites such as Barnes & Noble and Amazon use software to track reading preferences and actually recommend newly published books along the same genre. Why not employ intelligence gathering and use software to gently push specific venues? Even if your client doesn't use these recommendations, they certainly appreciate the offer.

Steps to Execution (S2E)

Now that you've captivated these clients with the front-end web site, delivering the brand promise is critical. The essence of a brand promise contains three parts: it's consistent, timely, and a perception of continued, future excellence. However you execute this process, the procured resources and logistics already exist and only require S2E. Conversely, miss any one of these components, however small, and the brand promise begins to unravel.

You can equate S2E to your next visit to Starbucks. You briskly walk in the door with a preconceived notation or brand promise—a venti Sumatra, which is both steaming hot and possessing a clean, yet flavorful, taste that lingers on your palate. Imagine if the S2E disintegrated for just one day. Was the coffee cold or too bitter? Did they change the music to a local hard rock station versus the usual relaxing jazz? Were the uniforms dirty or wrinkled?

To assure S2E, Starbucks provides their employees with a small manual called the "Green Apron Book," which details every nuance including values, daily mission, and attire. Both the work area and equipment are arranged to effectively deliver the brand promise despite the traffic flow or the time of day. In short, an intelligently designed process and communication system will ensure the brand promise will be executed each and every time.

Lessons Learned

In many ways, points of differentiation in the hotel industry become elusive because most competitors can quickly replicate short-term advantages. A recent article in one hotel magazine ran a story about kiosks as a preferred method for check-in/out by their patrons. Not unlike the airline industry, the ability to copy this capability equalizes any advantage and simply raises the standard and associated costs to do business.

The key to changing the rules of the game comes down to execution (S2E). Simply look to market leaders in varying industries. Dell offers the same computer hardware as Gateway and HP, but the market valuation resides in how Dell executes their strategy. The same holds true for Southwest Airlines. While every major carrier wallows in Chapter 11, Southwest just announced their 32nd consecutive profitable year. You decide!

The ability to create a disruption in any given market space comes down to two points: S2E and changing the rules of the game. Dell and Southwest took rather mundane industries and turned them into profitable market leaders. They, in effect, applied nano branding by identifying what people really value and creating a business model to serve that need. They took casual users and turned them into brand patriots. In short, the hotel and many other industries are just waiting for a company to do the same thing.

Summary

So, what did we learn here? We started by defining what a brand is from a historic point of view and sought insights from noted experts in industry and academia. Next, we considered various aspects of a brand: legacy, strategy, loyalty, and a new category, which I've coined nano brands. Taken together, we now have a sixty thousand foot view of what branding is and its business application.

Our objective was to provide an overview of brand principles. Not every concept or opinion could possibly be captured in this segment. The value in this broad brushstroke approach is to merely affirm notions concerning commonly held beliefs about this discipline.

Let's now turn our attention to a method to evaluate brands. The next chapter unveils the Brand Triad Theory and demonstrates its usefulness to the brand/marketing practitioner.

REFERENCE LIST

1 Handby, Terry. *Brands: Dead or Alive?* Journal of the Market Research Society. January, 1999.

2 Knapp, Duane. *The Brand Mindset.* McGraw-Hill, 1999.

3 Princeton University, www.cogsci.princeton.edu/cgi-bin/webwn

4. Merriam-Webster, http://www.m-w.com/cgi-bin/dictionary

5. Reeves, Rosser. *Reality in Advertising.* Mockingbird Books, 1961.

6. Kotler, Philip. *Marketing Management: Analysis, Planning, Implementation, and Control. Prentice Hall,* 1997.

7. Aaker, David. *Brand Portfolio Strategy.* Free Press, 2004.

8. Barnes, Beth. Shultz, Don. *Strategic Brand Communications Campaigns.* NTC Business Books, 1999.

9. Ries, Al. Trout, Jack. *The 22 immutable Laws of Branding.* Harper Business, 1993.

10. Davis, Scott. *Brand Asset Management: Driving profitable growth through your brands.* Jossey-Bass, 2002.

11. Bedbury, Scott. *A New Brand World.* Penguin, 2002.

12. Holt, Douglas. *How Brands Become Icons: The Principals of Cultural Branding.* Harvard Business School Press, 2004.

13. Barnes, Beth. Shultz, Don. *Strategic Brand Communications Campaigns.* NTC Business Books, 1999.

14. Christensen, Clayton. *Innovator's Solution.* Harvard Business School Press, 2003.

15. Zook, Chris. *Profit From The Core.* Harvard Business School Press, 2001.

16. Aaker, David. *Building Strong Brands.* The Free Press, 1996.

17. Christensen, Clayton. *Seeing What's Next.* Harvard Business School Press, 2004.

18. Bloemer J.M.M.; Kasper H.D.P.B. *The complex relationship between consumer satisfaction and brand loyalty.* Journal of Economic Psychology, Volume 16, Issue 2, 1995.

19. Trout, Jack. *Differentiate or Die: Survival in Our Era of Killer Competition.* John Wiley & Sons, 2000.

20. Hill, Sam. Lederer, Chris. *The Infinite Asset: Managing Brands to Build New Value.* Harvard Business School Press, 2001.

21. Lindstrom, Martin. *Brand Sense: Build Powerful Brands through Touch, Taste, Smell, Sight, and Sound.* Free Press, 2005.

Chapter Two

Brand Triad Concept

The journey to successful branding starts with a unique discernment of the value proposition being offered followed by vision, patience, and perseverance. By combining the latter mentioned acumens with a method of execution, organizations (i.e. brands) can emerge from the landscape of mediocrity.

The voyage from obscurity to trusted product or service occurs when assessing the three strategically positioned elements of the brand triad: attributes, behaviors, and circumstances. What significance do these elements have with great brands?

For starters, the lack of a solid foundation for a brand will ultimately undermine its future success. This foundation—attribute—goes beyond the logo and brand fascia and provides the underpinnings of legitimacy and ability to deliver real value. Thus, attributes are the mechanisms that enable a brand to function and carry out its purpose in commerce. An example might be the local video rental store: if they are constantly out of the newly released DVD titles, then a major attribute (rentals) of their existence diminishes in the consumer's mind, and they become less relevant as a future provider of entertainment.

Any product or service that we interact with on a daily basis must continuously pass this litmus test.

The type of reasoning that both buyer and seller share, which enables the basis or origin of a relationship, is the second characteristic— behaviors. Our behaviors as consumers are fickle at best and are in constant motion. How we behave on any given day may not ring true on another. As a provider of goods and services, the brand's owner must constantly understand the changing tides of tastes, desires, and preferences.

Finally, the setting by which attributes and behaviors are acted on must be appropriate in many respects. The circumstances by which we consume are in constant flux and subject to a myriad of conditional predispositions. The challenge for the brand in this regard is to identify patterns by which to insert an offering.

Shift in Attributes, Behaviors, and Circumstances

Consider mobile music devices: Sony Walkman was the main staple by which we consumed music in the 1990s. The benefit was choice: listening to either store-bought or homespun CDs while on the move. When a new offering (file-swapping of digital music on the Internet) was coupled with a device that was small, configurable, and stored thousands of songs appeared on the scene, a paradigm shift occurred in behavior. The rather cumbersome CD player and carrying case that held an assortment of plastic disks was now viewed as awkward and passé. The simplicity of a music hard drive allowed random access and sorting capabilities by music genre.

Thus, offering both the device and the ability to inexpensively acquire music on demand became a compelling consumable. Even the CEO of Sony, during a *60 Minutes* interview in 2006, admits missing this shift when considering the success of iTunes (digital music) and the iPod (device). In addition, the iPod was not the first mobile music device. A variety of other compact hard-drive players (disruptive technology) came on the scene, but each possessed a different platform (software and hardware) for MPEG downloads. It wasn't until the iPod bridged that gap by marrying desktop music management, online title access, hip design, and cool marketing to converge these elements into a great brand. It's not an easy undertaking, but studying the behavior of your core constituents provides insights into future consumption patterns.

Understanding Consumers Problems

A fairly recent article in *Harvard Business Review* discussed this very point (HBR, Dec '05). The example noted was consumption patterns of early morning commuters. The question posed in the article was how and why do consumers use milkshakes? On the surface, the fast-food retailer possessed basic information on top-line sales and traffic patterns. It was later revealed through qualitative research—interfacing with consumers—that the circumstances in which they consumed was based upon convenience, hunger abatement, and handling of the product. When the consumers were asked to compare milkshakes to other offerings such as bagels and doughnuts, the attributes of a thick substance contained in a cup (ease of use), and hunger satisfying effect were the compelling reasons for their selection. In this case, the circumstance—nourishment while you drive—was a powerful component to a brand selection and should alert marketing practitioners to better understand how consumers utilize their offerings.

Altogether, this concept suggests that a well-designed and executed brand triad may provide the basis for a well-positioned brand. This practical tool can assist the marketing/branding practitioner in analyzing their current position for each characteristic. Next, they can assess their desired position and the necessary steps to move in a more desirable direction. The outcome of this exercise can yield a set of tactical moves that will feed the overall brand strategy. The details of each leg of the triad will be covered in depth in the next section.

Brand Triad Constructs

Our next step delves into the building blocks and catalysts that make up this tool. This section attempts to bring definitions to these terms and create tangibles via a case study. To draw together all three characteristics at the end of this chapter, we'll use Southwest Airlines as an archetype to exemplify and support this concept.

Attributes

Whether you are discussing people, places, or things, attributes are the basis by which you compare, contrast, and distinguish levels of acceptance for use and consumption. Everything we do on a daily basis draws upon attributes to discern and validate who we are and our place on this earth. Why do you buy a certain car, brand of clothing, or a cup of coffee? Additionally, why do you connect with certain associates, friends, and neighbors? Conversely, why do you reproof, reject, and distance yourself from other products or services? Whether we want to admit it or not (intellectual versus emotional), we rely on associations—brands—that surround the attributes of people, places, and things.

I recently queried a highly educated associate of mine and asked why he drove a certain brand of automobile. Being an engineer, his response was both highly analytical and quantifiable: he supported his logic with facts such as miles-per-gallon, weight-to-horsepower, and the practical use to get him from point A to point B. When he was asked why he didn't buy a smaller, less expensive brand that could do the same job, his response was, "I wouldn't be caught *dead* in that car!" Touché.

Let's explore attributes on a slightly deeper level. The word attribute, according to *Merriam-Webster Dictionary*[3], is defined as:

1: an inherent characteristic; *also*: an accidental quality

2: an object closely associated with or belonging to a specific person, thing, or office <a scepter is the *attribute* of power>; *especially*: such an object used for identification in painting or sculpture

3: a word ascribing a quality

The word "inherent" coupled with "an object closely associated with…a specific person, thing, or office" has great significance. As you can see, these terms closely resemble my definition of attributes. Two concepts have been raised here that are worthy of discussion.

A research paper written by Michael Gassar in conjunction with Indiana University explores this concept of attributes. Gassar states that "nouns by themselves are limited in what things they allow us to distinguish." He suggests that "things" in our world have a value on a set of dimensions that describe such things as shapes, colors, smells, and tastes. He illustrates by use of a simple example: the apple. The category apple contains a "whole cluster of co-occurring features," asserts Gassar, and requires coherent categories for further definition.

Gassar goes on to state "the members of a category as having particular properties that Gassarcalls attributes. Each attribute is really a value on some dimension such as size, color, or consistency." He suggests that people have the ability to separate attributes from a category. "A small, sour apple isn't just an undifferentiated object for us. It's an apple, it's small, and it's sour."

In short, attributes are imperatives in our daily discrimination process, and they form the basis by which we make choices. Attributes alone will not satisfy anyone. To form such perceptions, there must be a foundation and process by which these attributes are executed and delivered. In the following aspect of the brand triad, we will examine the foundations that create a strong bond between perception and reality. The old adage seems to hold true: we shop intellectually but we purchase emotionally. Next, we will consider behavior in response to attributes and what that means to us as consumers.

Behaviors

Would you consider yourself a rational consumer? Most of us would answer yes. Interestingly, what we do and how we do it often defies reasonable thought despite our best intentions.

Several years ago, I attended a speaking engagement hosted by Tom Peters. During his presentation, he broached the topic of human behavior and mentioned a personal experience he had at the grocery store. Despite his high level of education (two Master's degrees and a PhD) and logical thought process, when he attempted to buy generic table salt at the store, he ended up purchasing the Morton Salt brand (blue label, little girl, and umbrella). He admittedly couldn't bring himself to buy the white-labeled, store brand (emotional) even though he (intellectually) believes that salt is salt, regardless of the package it comes in.

Don't we all behave the same way? You walk into a store to buy a can of soup. You see two products on the shelf: one has a no-name white label, the other is red with the brand name Campbell's written on it. Which one would you buy? Remember, the type of reasoning that both buyer and seller share enables the basis of a relationship. As a consumer, you are buying more than a can of soup, and this purchase reflects who you are (at the cash register), the perceived quality you provide your family (brand trust), and what you deem as acceptable in your world (values). This synergy between behavior and attributes, however contrived, becomes the paradigm by which we consume. Let's once again turn to noted research in an attempt to understand human behavior.

One such concept which analyzes how individuals interpret events and relate those events to their thinking and behavior is called attribution theory[4]. This groundbreaking work was developed by Fritz Heider in 1958 and further developed by both Jones and Weiner in the late 70s and 80s and became a bedrock of social psychology.

The essence of Heider's concept lies in what he calls surface events.[5] These are facets of social life that are intuitive and seemingly obvious to all. The importance here is to understand how someone behaves and what attributed to that behavior. Three key points here are

1) Perception or observation of the behavior

2) Intention of the behavior

3) Cause of the behavior

Marketers could gain greater insight into the attributes/behavior relationship by observing *how* people actually behave versus *what* people say they do (i.e., surveys). If you asked owners of CD players how to improve this product, they probably wouldn't have come up with the iPod concept. If you observe *how* they use CD players, their behavior would speak volumes about the gap that exists between the current offering and a desired solution (i.e., a runner's need for mobile music devices). Having discussed two aspects of the brand triad, let's see how they relate to circumstances.

Circumstances

The circumstances surrounding how we make purchasing decisions are situational at best. As a marketer, you may have the right attributes and behavior in place, but if the setting isn't appropriate, the whole concept falls apart. Let's discuss the auto industry as an example.

Buyers were seeking the next generation consumer vehicle, and being "green" was the latest rage. Automobile companies possessed the same relative resources, processes, and values to compete fairly for this emerging market. The attributes of design, functionality, and capability preexisted along with the behavior of consumers to continuously improve their driving experience while being environmentally friendly.

However, the problem for one auto company came into play with circumstances: the general public wasn't prepared to give up their gas-guzzling cars for a sub-compact, range-limited electric vehicle (EV) that this company had so heavily invested in. This same company then invested in hydrogen-powered vehicles, only to switch to hybrid in the end. As noted on Wikipedia, "In late 2003, GM officially canceled the EV1 program. Despite unfulfilled waiting lists and positive feedback from the lessees, GM stated that it could not sell enough of the cars to make the EV1 profitable. In fact, during the later stages of development for the car, GM officials claimed that they stood no chance of ever making a profit on the EV1 itself."

The technology of EVs under the current circumstances was not a good fit at that particular time, and, as a result, the electric vehicle product offering died a timely death. Conversely, Japanese automakers such as Toyota and Honda took the next, logical step and created a hybrid (gas/electric) vehicle that was closer to a standard car but with all the benefits of high mileage and environmental friendliness. Also, this hybrid technology didn't require the consumer to change their buying habits (i.e., use of gasoline).

What valuable lesson was learned? Although people desire higher mileage vehicles (attributes/behavior), the idea of a car that relies solely on battery technology—charge each night, limited range, and very small size—defies the circumstances of mainstream consumers. This was further compounded by the lack of accessible charging stations throughout the nation. Even Henry Ford dealt with the same issue regarding his mass-produced Model T—neither a network of paved roads nor a proliferation of gas stations existed in that day to support his technology.

Example: Southwest Airlines

Now that we have defined the brand triad, let's apply it to a real-world setting. We begin with a product/service that most have used or are at least aware of: Southwest Airlines.

Attributes

The attributes of Southwest (SW) are straightforward: friendly, inexpensive, frequent flights, quick turns, fun flight attendants. On their web site, www.southwest.com, you'll see their mission statement mirrors reality:

> *"The mission of Southwest Airlines is dedication to the highest quality of Customer Service delivered with a sense of warmth, friendliness, individual pride, and Company Spirit."*

Under a section called "about us," they summarize their value proposition to the masses:

> *"More than 32 years ago, Rollin King and Herb Kelleher got together and decided to start a different kind of airline. They began with one simple notion: If you get your passengers to their destinations when they want to get there, on time, at the lowest possible fares, and make darn sure they have a good time doing it, people will fly your airline."*

Now that we understand their public persona, let's briefly understand the foundation that makes this actually work. In 1971, SW airline saw the landscape of this business as hub-and-spoke, expensive maintenance facilities, multiple aircraft, major airports, and expensive unions.

What was unique about SW from the start was the business model they pursued, which was contrary to the status quo. In effect, SW stayed away from major airports, used point-to-point service, purchased only one type of aircraft (737s), and cross-functionally trained their employees. They also considered what the traveling public viewed as important (see Figure six) and designed their offerings accordingly. By adjusting their business model, they reduced or eliminated those offerings the public didn't view as important and increased amenities they enjoyed. For the price-conscious traveler, food and comfort was of little value compared to on-time arrivals and a fun experience.

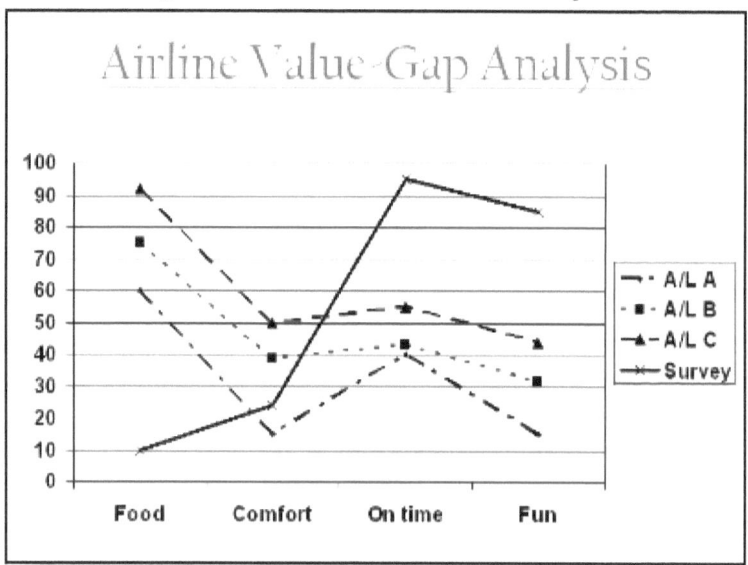

The outcome of this foundation provided
1.   A low-cost business model
2.   Low fares to consumers
3.   A profitable enterprise

The economics behind this business model appears simple, yet so many major carriers attempted to incorporate a competing design with little success. For example, United Airlines launched United Express as a method for attracting discount flyers. The problem was that their cost structure couldn't support discounted fares and, thus, became a losing proposition. Over twenty years, SW literally changed the rules of this game. A low-cost business model became the new standard for competition and spawned a similar company called Jet Blue. In short, the attributes of an intelligently designed business followed by impeccable execution makes SW a great brand.

Behaviors

What shared reasoning occurred between the general public and SW that formed the basis of a mutually beneficial relationship? Let's consider the following: SW provided less service, less amenities, and certainly less prestige than all other offerings in the commercial airline industry. Why would anyone want something less—isn't more supposed to be better?

During the nineties, the "do-it-yourself" phenomenon occurred, and companies such as Lowes and the Home Depot burst onto the scene. The Home Depot grew from 145 stores and $3.8 billion in sales in 1990 to 1890 stores and $73.1 billion in sales by 2004; they were named the most admired specialty retailer by *Fortune Magazine* in February 2005. Their corporate web site states:

> *"The Home Depot is committed to offering the ultimate home improvement shopping experience. With about 40,000 different products, trademark customer service and guaranteed low prices, The Home Depot stores cater to do-it-yourselfers and do-it-for-me's, as well as home improvement, construction and building maintenance professionals."*

Whether you are trying to reach a certain destination or fix a broken lawn sprinkler, the behavior remains the same. In both cases, people will actually accept less for a good price. The behavior has achieved balance with attributes—business model—for delivering what they want, when they want it, and for a discounted price. In both cases, these companies are organizationally excellent at the value they deliver!

Circumstances

Let's start this discussion with the concept of "under and overshooting" expectations. What does this mean? When you want to fly from Orange County, California, to New York, New York, you have many choices available. Not only does your range of options include a variety of carriers, but various levels of service. The middle of the road would consist of a fair price, a reasonably comfortable seat, and a palatable meal.

To overshoot this event, we would spend thousands on a first-class ticket, sit in a big leather seat, and eat a gourmet meal served on china tableware. To undershoot, we would sit in cramped seats, eat a bag of pretzels, and have more than two connections with unusually long layovers. The circumstances in which people fly vary depending on the dimensions presented. Since SouthWest's value proposition is so clear and forthright, passangers typically know in advance the experience they will receive.

In today's environment, the ability to rationalize value is primarily a function of available information. If you rely on a travel agent, your span of available dimensions is severely limited and reliant on the assessment of others. As with the travel agent, how far you under or overshoot your desired experience may never be known or will be discovered after the fact. Conversely, the Internet provides a wealth of options that allow the user to select attributes/circumstances and compare the results. In effect, our ability to determine the circumstances in which we travel, to a large extent, falls to the consumer. Next, we will draw these three concepts together. The following section presents this connection theoretically and conceptually.

Brand Triad Model: How It Functions

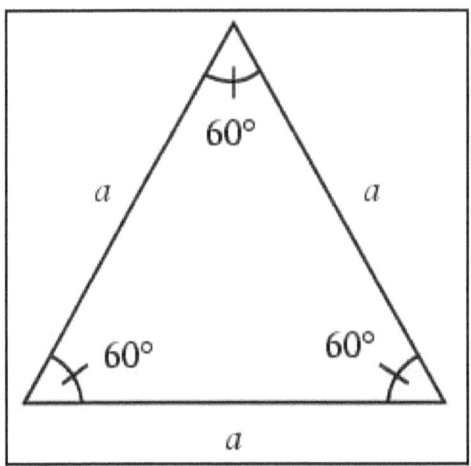

The purpose of this section is to discuss the functional components of this triangular-shaped brand model. We will start with a foundational understanding of this concept and then examine each of the three triangular components (legs) separately. Next, we will insert two variables on either end of each leg to examine how they interact with one another. Finally, we will combine the three legs into an equal-sided triangle and view the entire design. We are not attempting to create a new mathematical or scientific equation, but merely developing a functioning business model to conduct a brand assessment. This process (i.e., situational analysis) will then be used as input on the application of our brand model in chapter three.

A basic construct of the brand triad model pertains to levels of acceptability. In any given situation, we face choices (behavior) based on the availability (circumstances) of consumables (attributes). One way to articulate this is to use a measurement tool of some type. As consumers, we all convey our preferences in terms of good versus bad, or we apply some self-appointed scale such as one to ten, where ten is perfection. Whatever metric is used to express the level of acceptance, we do rate everything we consume.

Basic Triad Scale

For purposes of standardizing on a single metric, let's use a scale that reflects both good and bad experiences. In college, most of us were exposed to something called standard deviation. We are not attempting to apply standard deviation to this discussion. The only resemblance is to borrow this bell curve graph, which represents variance from the mean, or middle. Please refer to our scale below:

One way to apply our scale is to view any point away from zero as less desirable. The standard deviation model works much in the same manner. The center position would be the most preferred choice. As you move away from the center, the experience becomes less positive. This There are two sides to this scale for purposes of comparing and contrasting two variables.

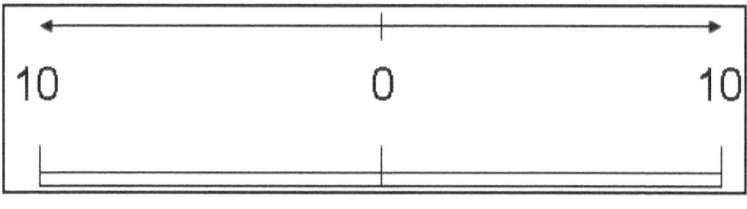

Less Desirable   Most Desirable   Less Desirable

Let's further define how this model operates by comparing attributes to circumstances using a widely known measurement device. The best analogy to demonstrate this concept is a simple weight scale. At one end of our scale, a consumer would assign a weight or value to a product/service (attributes). On the other end, our consumer would assign a weight or value to the way in which he or she consumes (circumstances). Our continual goal as consumers is to achieve a balance between attributes and circumstances in any given situation. Should the weight on either side of the scale change, the scale will shift direction (up or down) and will be out of balance. The brand triad scale, on the other hand, is a linear tool that shifts from the center toward one direction or the other. Once this occurs, our linear scale is out of balance.

Let's try an example to see how this scale functions. You go to your favorite restaurant to eat dinner. We've anchored one side of our scale with attributes and the other end with circumstances. A perfect meal would be in position zero. Anything less than perfect would move away from the zero position—less desirable experience, although still positive. You may say you had an ok meal, but would probably return at a later date with the anticipation of experiencing perfection. In your mind's eye, zero is perfect, five is ok, and ten is definitely bad.

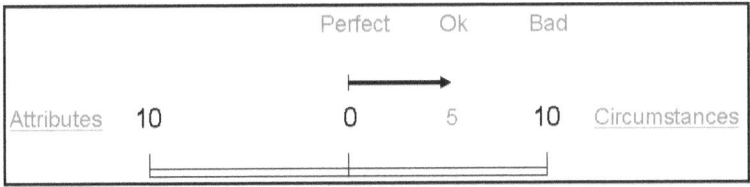

What's happening here? The attributes of our restaurant include ambiance, taste, service, selection, and other product/service values. If our starting position is zero, or perfection, cold food, a rude waiter, or a long wait in line, despite our reservation, would move us *away* from the desired attributes of this restaurant and, thus, generate a negative experience. The degree of negativity—how far we move from center—depends on how bad the experience was.

You are probably wondering why another complex scale for measuring consumer behavior is needed? The short answer is to compare and contrast two variables. Because there are three constituents, or legs, an equilateral triangle worked well to connect any point to the other two. In this manner, you can compare attributes to both circumstances and behavior. The following examples apply this scale and illustrate its intended use.

Chocolate Bar Scenario: Attributes

When comparing attributes to behaviors, the level of product preference varies depending on the strength of our desires. I desire a Hershey's chocolate bar, so I walk from my office to the vending machine down the hall. After reviewing all the offerings, there are a limited number of chocolate bars available, and my core brand, Hershey's, is sorely absent. Because my desire for chocolate remains strong, I select something close to the core idea—chocolate coating, not solid—and derive some level of satisfaction. As illustrated in Figure 11 I moved away from product attributes—most desirable to least—and towards a modified behavior: Snickers, not Hershey's.

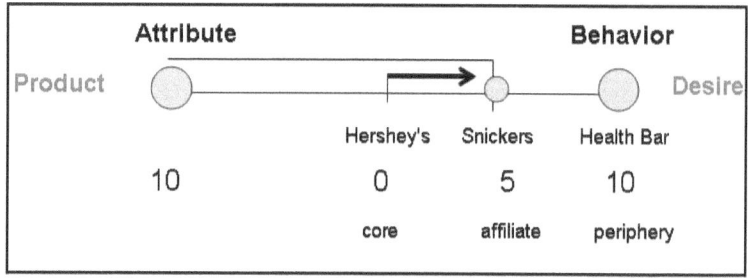

Observations

Two simultaneous events occurred during the decision-making process. First, when a core brand was not available, I sought a substitute that resembled the core idea. In this example, an affiliate brand, Snickers, was considered the closest (attribute) to our desired selection. Although my preference was a solid milk chocolate bar, none of the others chocolate offerings were deemed acceptable.

In some cases, the only option drifts far (periphery) from the core and vaguely resembles the original idea (like a chocolate-coated health bar). In our new position, we move away from preferred product attributes and toward our desire in a less desirable form (negative shift). Our new plot, (15A, 5B), demonstrates the individual's thought process.

How did we arrive at these numerical plot points, you may ask? If you refer back to Figure 11, we moved away from the preferred product attributes by 15 points: ten was derived from the distance between attribute and the core plus five additional points from the core to our affiliate position. From a behavior standpoint, we digressed five points from the core.

We fulfilled our desire for chocolate, but the cost to do so garnered a negative experience. If you were the owner of the vending machine, perhaps an employee survey might help to uncover collective tastes and preferences. With the advent of electronics and microprocessors, collecting valuable insights into brand preferences could be integrated into the selection process. As a consumer, my ability to voice my displeasure that a Hershey's chocolate bar as not available helps both the vendor and brand owner. Let's now consider product attributes as they relate to circumstances.

Chocolate Bar Scenario: Circumstances

The circumstances in which we consume may dictate how far we will go to achieve satisfaction. When comparing attributes to circumstances, the perfect situation would result in acquiring a Hershey's bar from the vending machine down the hall. If the vending machine option fails, we either accept a substitute or forego the chocolate bar experience altogether. In this scenario, our desire for the core brand (attribute) is so compelling that we will leave the office and drive down the street to a local gas station. In this manner, seeking the core brand will have a negative effect due to the effort exerted to achieve satisfaction.

	Attribute			Circumstance
Product	○	○ ←——————		○ Situation
	Grocery Store	Gas Station	Vending	
	10	5	0	10
	periphery	affiliate	Core	

Observations

Achieving balance between attributes and circumstances in a given situation is always preferred. When a core brand is not readily available, we change our circumstances to achieve satisfaction. In this example, an affiliate location is the perceived solution. In our new position, we moved *away* from preferred circumstances—the office vending machine—and drove to the gas station down the street. Although the core brand has been acquired, we went out of our way to derive satisfaction. Our new plot, (5A, 15C), demonstrates a strong brand preference, but due to its locale, produced a negative experience. Let's now compare behavior to circumstances.

Chocolate Bar Scenario: Behavior

Sometimes our behavior may change as it pertains to circumstances. Consider this situation: We are at work, hungry, and unable to leave the office to acquire our core brand: Hershey's. Because the vending machine offerings are deemed unacceptable, we shift our preferences to items that will satisfy both our hunger and sweet-tooth. In this case, an affiliate product may be cookies.

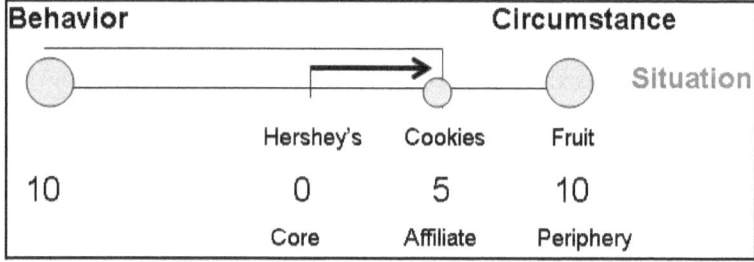

Observations

Achieving balance between behavior and circumstances in a given situation may not occur and may require a shift in product attributes. When a core brand is not readily available, we change our behavior to achieve some level of satisfaction. In effect, we moved *away* from our desired solution, and cookies were deemed a close substitute to a Hershey's bar, given the current circumstances. Our new position becomes (15B, 5C). We achieve some level of satisfaction with the cookies, but it carries with it a negative affect.

Summation

In the previous examples, we presented three facets of the brand triad model and its basic functionality. This was accomplished by successfully comparing and contrasting each segment: A–B, A–C, and B–C. In each scenario, we applied a setting (at work, vending machine) with a given situation (hunger, sweet tooth, and desire for a core brand). By capturing the outcomes and placing the information on a scattergram (see Figure 14, we can quickly assess consumption patterns (shaded area) based on the information provided.

	Hershey's Scenario					
	10	5	0	5	10	
Attributes						Behavior
Attributes						Circumstances
Behavior						Circumstances

Let's summarize our findings:

1) I shifted away from a core brand to a close facsimile (A–B)

2) I inconvenienced myself to acquire a core brand (A–C)

3) I shifted from a core brand to an entirely different product category (B–C)

In each of the three scenarios, my core brand was unavailable and, thus, forced me to modify acceptable attributes, alter my circumstances, or change my behavior to a different product offering. The significance of this method is to understand the consumption patterns of individuals based on these three constructs. If I was a brand manager for Hershey's, this type of information would be useful to enhance future marketing strategies. For example, if the vending machine could collect data on purchases, a brand manager could assess what items were purchased after the core brand inventory was exhausted. Next, we can broaden our view from an individual's preference to a larger audience.

Let's imagine we surveyed all one thousand employees that had access to the same vending machine and a appropriate percentage of the population possessed a preference for the Hershey brand. In addition, suppose our linear model had ten possibilities (adjectives or descriptors) for each position on our scale (from core to periphery). We can now query all employees using the three scenarios above. The value in this exercise is to assess how consumers, employees in this case, view a given core brand as it pertains to attributes, behaviors, and circumstances. Moreover, it also should provide insights into alternative actions, such as affiliate or periphery products and services. The hypothetical outcomes might look something like this (see Figure 15).

When comparing products (attributes) to desires (behavior), these employees selected an offering that was very close to the core brand. The concentration of surveyed responses is noted on a grey scale: black illustrates high a concentration of responses, medium grey reflects moderate, light grey reflects sparse feedback, and no response is indicated by a white space.

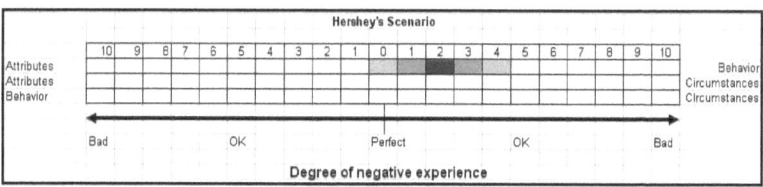

The highest concentration of responses, noted on position two (2), reflects the survey adjective "great" and was associated with "achieving fulfillment for chocolate of some type." When asked if the experience was negative, the general feeling was "not negative, but less than desired product." To summarize attributes to behavior, our control group sought a Hershey's bar (core idea) and then shifted to an affiliate offering in lieu of no chocolate: (12A, 8B).

When comparing products (attributes) to a given situation (circumstances), these employees viewed an off-site acquisition of their core brand as not preferred. The primary concentration of responses, as noted by position one, demonstrates that they are unwilling to leave the office to seek the core brand. More important than the actual number should be the reasons behind such a reaction. The two common responses, as unveiled through qualitative interviews, indicate time and effort are the mitigating factors.

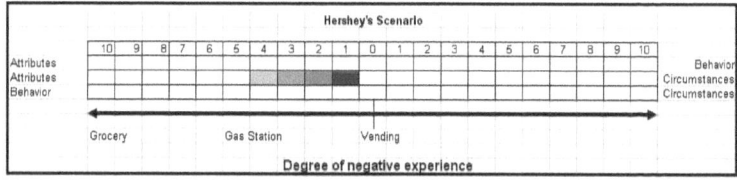

A great percentage of workers surveyed—85 percent—are hourly employees with breaks at designated times. They have only enough time to walk to the break room and enjoy a snack while conversing with fellow workers. The professional staff—15 percent—on the other hand, doesn't adhere to set breaks and meanders to the break room at their own discretion. It's clear that neither hourly nor salary employees would seek the core brand off-site. Only a small percentage, light grey at position four, would make the effort to drive to the gas station for the core brand, and this primarily constitutes the professional staff members.

Our final scenario compares behavior to circumstances. The survey questions center on alternate behavior when the core brand is not available. Employees were asked to stand in front of the vending machine and verbalize their decision-making process. Starting from the top and working their way to the offerings on the lowest level, they explained why most of the products didn't suit their needs. Because their core brand—Hershey's—was not available, most employees surveyed shifted from chocolate bars to cookies and other sweetened products.

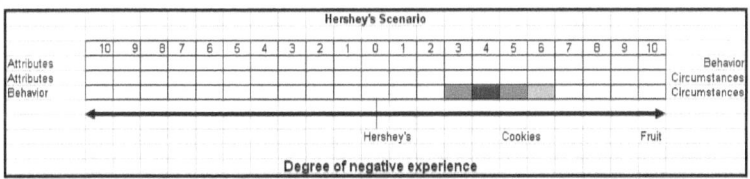

When asked if this was a negative experience, most agreed that, because they desired chocolate, sweet snacks and cookies were a poor substitute. In this case, most of the control group changed their behavior based on the circumstances and made alternate product choices (changed category).

Outcomes

This section was dedicated to understanding how the brand triad functions. The overarching purpose was to create a brand assessment tool based on how consumers actually behave when faced with three common variables: attributes, behaviors, and circumstances. What consumers—whether business-to-business, business-to-consumer, or consumer to consumerarticulate versus their actions may differ. The challenge facing marketing practitioners comes in the form of how their target audience acts versus what survey data leads them to believe.

The common question my colleagues pose at this juncture is "How can I apply this to my business?" Consider how the brand triad model could be utilized in the following scenario:

Business: Component manufacturer

Channel: Direct sales to Original Equipment Manufacturers (B2B)

Medium: Direct mail, advertisements, web, and trade shows

Competition: Several like competitors offering similar products

Pricing: Acceptable margins, could be better

Let's start with attributes. Let's assume this component manufacturer produces a quality product with on-time delivery and other notable industry requirements. In competitive situations, they rely on these attributes as the backbone of their offering. To understand what challenges they face and how they can help, they frequently visit valuable customers. On the surface, typical responses center on higher quality, faster delivery, and better pricing. Nothing new here, right?

You shift to behavior. For the most part, your customers operate in much the same manner as you do. Whether they are buyers, engineers, quality, or business development, these roles are typically trying to solve the same problems as you do on a daily basis. Each discipline has their specific desires, and they look to industry to solve them. So far, you've uncovered nothing significant.

Last, you shift to circumstances. In a recent interview, Clayton Christensen of Harvard Business School proclaims…

*"We always have an overwhelming tendency to frame the market we are targeting by the boundaries defined by product categories, or product points, or the demographics of the customers. We think about industry verticals. When we target products that markets that are defined by demographics of customers or by the product's characteristics, we are playing the crapshoot game of determining whether or not there is a valid customer need. We define our business as helping a customer get a job done—one that he is already struggling to get done and has no satisfactory means of doing so—the probability that product will contact with the customer is very high. **You need to look at what is the customer trying to get done and does your product or service help that customer get it done better**. Or, does it make it easier for them to do what they aren't trying to get done. The latter is a failure."*

During in-depth discussions with your key customers, a circumstance unfolds that piques your interest. Unbeknownst to you or your sales force, a hidden problem emerged that your customers have been trying to solve for some time. Not only are they dedicating vast resources to solve this particular problem, but the amount of scrap generated has grave implications on their bottom line. Bingo! You take this valuable information back to your office and map your brand triad.

Triad Mapping

You start with attributes to behavior and conclude that there resides a balance, for most situations, between these two variables. Next, you consider behavior to circumstances and assess that these two variables are in check. Based on what you just learned, you now consider attributes to circumstances. You send out your sales force to confirm this situation with like customers, and they report back unanimously: Yes!

The next step is to quantify the distance from a point of balance— zero—to the customer's current state. As with the Hershey's chocolate example, you find a scattering of responses and a high concentration around a number or descriptor. Your next step is to consider the cost associated with solving this particular problem for the customer. It may include a minor adjustment to your offering for which you can now charge a premium. As the brand or marketing practitioner, you can now adjust your strategy for this specific market and leverage this knowledge for growth and increased profitability. You position your brand strategy to address this problem, and the messaging demonstrates how they can achieve equilibrium (solution). This scenario is no different than what Apple's iPod did to Sony's CD player. It was the same attributes–circumstances, or product and use, that enabled the new entrant to cripple the incumbent. The iPod, in effect, changed the rules as it pertained to mobile music. Why shouldn't your company take advantage of the same philosophy and uncover a hidden value that could increase revenues and profitability?

A Second Dimension

In addition to comparing two variables, the brand Triad employs a second, vertical, dimension. Up to this point, we have only considered the horizontal axis and anchored a variable on either end of the segment to draw a comparison. As in the real world, we can connect or disconnect with our brands at any given time. What does this mean?

A simple example could be a product that was always available in the vending machine. If it is always there then we have achieved a balance between attributes and circumstances. If the vending company stops carrying our product, a disconnect suddenly occurs. Our center point that was nicely situated between attributes and circumstances separates from our continuum (leg). Another way to express this event is that the attributes and circumstance are in balance, but the product is missing. Our point shifts neither toward attributes nor circumstances in a linear fashion because we are in balance (right desire, right place). Therefore, our point falls off the line between A–C. A disconnect has occurred between the consumer and a given brand because the ability for a commercial transaction fails to transpire.

Conversely, we can view the depth of brand loyalty by moving away from the continuum and towards the apex of the triangle. The following discussion explains this concept and considers how connected we are to certain brands.

Application of Second Dimension

So far, we have established a linear movement or position on a continuum of each leg. The functionality of how a point was determined helped us assess how consumers make decisions. Once a plot has been made between two variables (ex. attribute/behavior), a second dimension must be determined. For example, if there resides a balance between the two, the next step is to determine the degree of connection (engagement) with their choice.

Figure 18 illustrates one of the three triangular segments, or legs. This particular segment was anchored by two variables, as previously demonstrated. A second dimension was added to each leg that includes a vertical scale from ten to zero. The arrow points towards the apex of this triangle: a preferred position. Thus (0,0) illustrates a perfect match between A–B. As you can see, this connection line slopes downward as you reach either end of the A–B range (position ten). This simply means that as the vertical arrow moves away from the center, the consumer was less connected with the product or service. Also, the degree of satisfaction becomes more limited as you move toward the ten position on the horizontal. In essence, when you are positioned at ten on the horizontal between attribute/behavior, it naturally follows that a corresponding vertical position nearing ten will also occur.

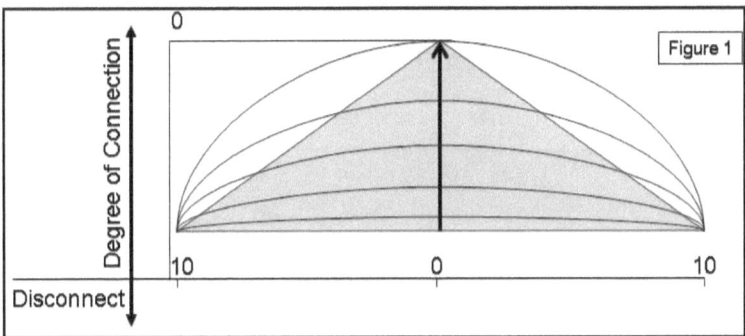

Application

For example, you may strike a balance between a product and desire, but if the product attributes fail in any regard, such as being unavailable, our new position moves off the line and a disconnection occurs. Conversely, should the product exceed our expectations, such as superior service at a hotel, the plot point moves toward the center position. The deeper the connection with the brand and the more excellent the experience, the closer to the center our position becomes (see the section on nano brands). Perfect harmony is zero on the horizontal and zero on the vertical

Let's return to our first scenario. We desired a Hershey's bar but settled for a Snickers (dot at 15A, 5B). Using our survey metrics (adjectives assigned to each number), we view this experience as a five, or ok, in our mind's eye. We have settled on our horizontal position. Next, we want to know the degree of satisfaction. Our position naturally shifts upward on the vertical scale. On our scale of ten to zero, zero being optimal, the connection achieved can be measured by the individual. As noted on the curve below, our level of satisfaction resides at position four on the vertical. You can also see from the graph that our level of satisfaction has limitations. This simply means, in this scenario, the maximum vertical number achievable is five.

To summarize, this consumer shifted away from the brand and toward an affiliate offering. This generated a negative experience. In addition, some level of satisfaction was achieved by acquiring a facsimile of the core brand. Our new plot point is five on the vertical and (15A, 5B) on the horizontal.

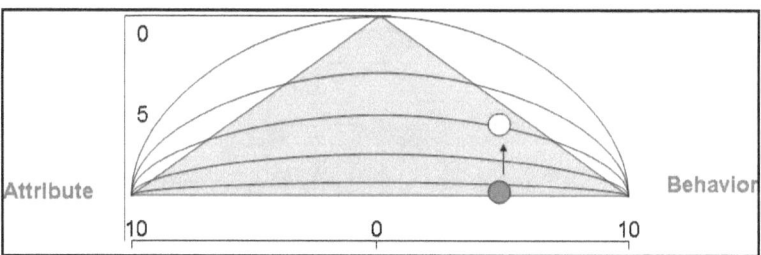

So, what do these plot points and numbers really mean to a brand manager? Moreover, how would a marketing practitioner apply this model to their given business scenario? The next chapter assembles the three segments and demonstrates its overall functionality in a hypothetical scenario.

Brand Triad Summary

Before we move on, let's recap the material presented thus far and summarize the overall brand triad process. To apply this model to your specific business, you would first compare your products or service attributes to how people actually behave. Using customer focus groups, surveys, and other qualitative and quantitative data, determine if the attributes are in balance with the audience's actual behavior (zero on the A–B line is perfect harmony). This critical step should not be glossed over or given to a lower-level functionary to analyze. Don't assume you know how your customers think. Your entire future trajectory depends on this first, very important step. If you don't dig deep enough or uncover what real-world problem your potential customers are trying to solve, all subsequent actions you take will lead you down the wrong path—a very costly misstep.

Recall the milk shake example. To the owners, they were marketing this product to children as a lunch or after school drink. In reality, their most frequent consumers were adults who opted for a convenient, hunger abatement snack over more traditional breakfast items such as bagels, donuts, and fruit during their drive to work. These consumers shifted on the A–B scale from a traditional breakfast snack to a periphery product, the milk shake. The circumstance of driving to work while handling an awkwardly shaped or messy breakfast item was the problem to be solved. In addition, the contents, a thick substance, fended off hunger for a longer period of time. After the owners truly understood this A–B phenomenon, product extensions emerged— milk shakes with fruit and other ingredients—to adapt to this new and growing niche market. Unless you truly uncover the root cause of the problem, your efforts will be in vain.

Real World Application

Not to belabor this point, but many years ago I was working with a very bright and educated engineer on a new product offering. His assumption, which was manifested through many customer engagements, was to marry two technologies together. Through this process, he asked leading questions to his client base and typically received responses that supported his hypothesis. This lack of objectivity and insight when surveying your constituents can lead you astray.

Despite my misgivings about this new product combination, he sold the CEO on the concept and actually won several internal technology innovation awards for his creation. After following a prescribed product development process, he launched the offering into the marketplace and heavily promoted it in the press and at industry-related trade shows. Despite their best efforts, this new offering generated only a few sample orders but no real business.

Assessment

Let's use the brand triad model to assess what went wrong. According to the survey data and customer affirmations, the attributes of the offering and behavior were in check: technology and desired use. Similar products were selling in the marketplace for a comparable price, and the intended use of the product was equivalent. Next, the attributes to the circumstances seemed in balance: what the product did for the given application. If you placed this model next to the competition, you would have a hard time deciding which product worked best. Although the latter two segments were in balance, the product didn't sell. What happened? Let's examine the behavior–circumstances leg of the brand triad.

The marketplace offered a myriad of these devices in various sizes and levels of sensitivities. This new combination possessed similar capabilities in a comparable package and price point. On the surface, this new offering could be substituted for any incumbent product. All things being equal, this emergent product should have acquired some market share, enjoyed normal product life cycle revenues, and amassed reasonable margins.

As it turned out, the product line limped along for four years and was later sold to a competing firm. The product never recovered its research and development investment and lost money year after year. The combination technology wasn't the problem—it turned out to be the behavior associated with the circumstance (B–C). This product required an annual calibration adjustment, and incumbents possessed a network of local houses that supported this vital function. Because this firm lacked that key ingredient, and their offering was unsupported by existing calibration houses, the product was viewed as a liability. In essence, the engineer who selectedthis product had to assume that responsibility and develop internal resources to support field calibrations. In short, if all three legs of the brand triad were analyzed during the discovery phase of the product development process, this technology combination would have been abandoned.

To summarize, when analyzing your current offering or new product development initiatives, begin by establishing the A–B point, and then repeat this process for the two remaining lines: A–C and B–C (see Figure 20. As previously discussed, it is possible that a point can fall outside of the line or disconnect from the continuum. To illustrate this point, let's use a Starbucks store and the A–C line as an example. The attributes (coffee) and behavior (desire) for this establishment are highly desirable, but this outlet (which was conveniently situated on your way to work each morning) was suddenly closed. This event prevented an interaction or purchase to take place, and a disconnect occurred between your audience and your offering. As a result, the point on the A–C line will fall outside of the triangle.

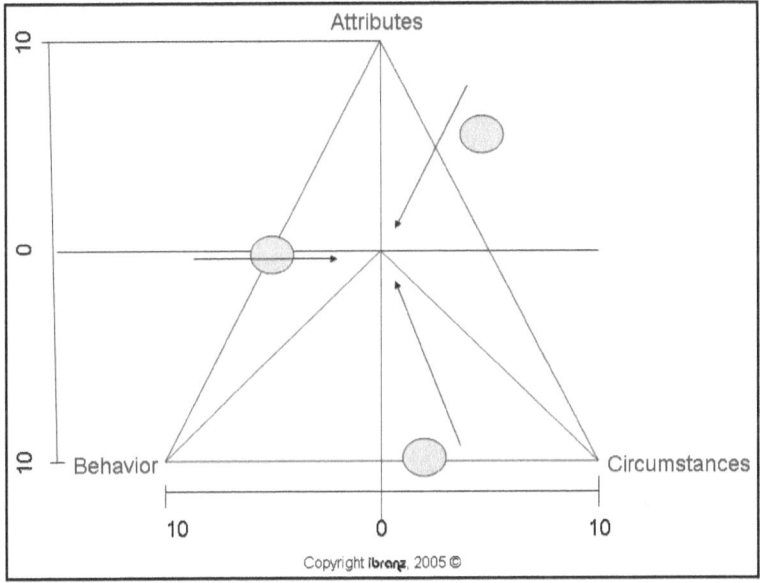

Copyright Ibrand, 2005 ©

Disconnects occur all the time and for many reasons. During the latter part of the year, Starbucks offers pumpkin scones along with a vast assortment of other baked goods. I wait all year to buy one and will go out of my way, which means driving to several stores, to locate them. The difference between the latter example and a coffeehouse closure is significant. The obvious reason is that one is seasonal and the other is a daily event. You may still prefer the Starbucks brand, but you will move toward an adjacent offering for convenience sake. As humans, our expectations vary depending on the circumstances.

Now that you have plotted all three points, consider the depth to which the consumer owns your brand. The center point (0,0) defines perfect balance of all three constituents—arrows moving toward the center. The beauty of plotting your current state and considering a desired position is that it will allow you to visualize what needs to be accomplished and it helps refine your brand strategy

What constitutes a powerful brand? By applying the concept of a brand triad, we are able to assess the current state of the brand's attributes, behaviors, and circumstances. Through this process, we attempt to answer the question of what problem is the customer trying to solve? By analyzing each segment of the triad, we are able to determine if our offering addresses this issue in a unique way. You may need to repeat this process for different channels, geographic locations, cultures, and special situations.

In closing, this tool was developed to help the marketing practitioner visualize his or her brand(s) current position and consider a future state, or trajectory. Through this process, the viability of a product or service in a given situation may become more transparent. Also, it may uncover potential liabilities that exist in the initial marketing strategy. The dynamics of the plotted points on the brand triad are in constant motion due to market forces and competitive moves, and they may require annual evaluations. Taken together, the opportunity to formulate or redesign a relevant brand resides in the hands of business leaders each day.

REFERENCE LIST

1. 60 minutes (CBS News), "**Sir Howard Stringer: Sony's Savior?**" **January 8, 2006,** http://www.cbsnews.com/stories/2006/01/06/60minutes/main1183023.shtml

2. Christensen, Clayton. *Marketing Malpractice: The Cause and the Cure.* Harvard Business Review, 2005.

3. Merriam-Webster Dictionary Online http://www.merriam-webster.com/

4. Indiana University and Michael Gasser. Attributes and attribution www.indiana.edu/~hlw/Composition/attribution.html Edition 2.0, 23, Mar, 2003

5. Heidler, Fritz. The Psychology of Interpersonal Relations. Contributors: Fritz Heider - author. Publisher: Lawrence Erlbaum Associates, 1958.

6. Wikipedia, http://en.wikipedia.org/wiki/General_Motors_EV1

7. Southwest Airlines, http://www.southwest.com/about_swa/mission.html

8. Home Depot, http://corporate.homedepot.com/wps/portal/!ut/p/.cmd/cs/.ce/7_0_A/.s/7_0_10J/_s.7_0_A/7_0_10J

Chapter Three

Brand Triad Application

Let's now apply the brand triad model. Multiple examples haven been offered for parts, this time its being applied in its entirety. Rather than conjure up a safe scenario, it might be more interesting to pick a troubled marketplace where highly-educated minds are struggling on a daily basis to solve an industry-wide dilemma. You are the new vice president of marketing for XYZ Airline. This regional airline covers the western states, owns one hundred seventy-five aircraft, and has annual sales of $800 million. In your new role, you have been given the following three assignments:

1) Assess the current landscape of the domestic airline marketplace

2) Determine value gaps and opportunities for growth

3) Provide strategic recommendations to the CEO

As part of your toolkit, you begin by utilizing a framework termed RPV (Christensen/Raynor, 2003) to determine the most appropriate business model design under the current conditions. This sixty thousand foot view assesses *resources*, *process*, and *value* of your organization and those of your competitors. Next, by applying the brand triad model, you will assess both your current and future state to identify the types of changes XYZ will need to implement. The outcome of this exercise will yield a definable brand strategy and recommendation to your CEO.

Historic Background

The state of the commercial airline industry during the post-war era was indeed optimistic. An expansion in routes, faster aircraft (DC–3, Constellation, etc.), and disposable incomes drove the trajectory of this business. As a result, heavy investment in new aircraft (jet age, greater distance, food service) and expanded services became the new standard of competition. These actions, in turn, created a hub-and-spoke approach with maintenance hubs (unions) to handle multiple aircraft repairs. The outlook for this high-growth market was stellar throughout the 1960s. The amenities and associated costs moved up market from rudimentary offerings to match what was perceived as the new consumer paradigm.

Airlines, once protected in a regulated world (ending in 1978), then had to face the grim reality of labor disputes and the new era of discount fares. The recession of the 1970s challenged this once profitable industry with increased competition, soaring fuel prices, filling seats, and carrying heavy debt. In order to afford these high, fixed costs, most airlines relied on profitable business travelers to offset discounted fares. A long list of airlines failed this test: Eastern Airlines, People's Express, Pan Am, TWA, and many others.

Current State: 2008

Today's landscape involves heavy competition and increasing oil prices (nearing $150 a barrel). If you survey the top airlines, most have recently emerged from Chapter 11 and are struggling to make a profit. To survive, they are reducing employee wages, selling routes, and eliminating the funding of pension plans. Only one airline, Southwest, who redefined this industry during the 1980s, has created a business model which suits both the prevailing financial and consumer requirements (circumstances/behavior).

In late 2007, a major newspaper reported that "option traders hinted at airlines consolidation by buying call options on three carriers." This *Wall Street Journal* article noted that heavy buying of March calls for Northwest Airlines, Delta Airlines, and UAL Corp where under way. According to this November 27, 2007 *Wall Street Journal* article, "Pardis Capital Management LP, an investor in both Delta Air Lines Inc. and United Airlines parent UAL Corp., this month took public its proposal that the two airlines merge. Despite the regulatory and operational obstacles to a merger, this hedge fund is trying to rally support amongst like-minded investment firms to follow suit. The rationale espoused includes a hedge against higher fuel prices and economic down turn."

At the same time, Southwest Airlines appeared to be augmenting its basic strategy from no frills to adding a preferential boarding option termed "Business Select." Southwest CEO Gary Kelly characterized this shift in business model design as not abandoning discount travel but merely updating it. The reasoning behind this shift includes the equalizing of the low-cost equation—over time, low cost competition and larger carriers have reduced this gap. Other carriers have focused on the business fliers that are willing to pay more for such amenities. Southwest would like to tap a portion of the business flier market by offering such preferential service for $10 to $30 more each way. Despite the fact that 40 percent to 50 percent of their customer base is last minute business travelers, they would like to capture the high revenues associated with this market.

The looming question for Southwest is will they offend their loyal customer base by changing their value proposition? The previous site had five options for the discount traveler to choose from. Today, this has been narrowed down to three selections: Business, Business Select, and Wanna Get Away. According to the November 27th *Wall Street Journal* article, Mr. Kelly said the changes are about passenger choice. Consumers perceptions are hard to change, and this migration might be a logical step for Southwest, but it may offend 50 percent of their customer base at the same time. This dissatisfaction may leave a window open for the next disruptive, low-cost airline.

In December 2007, a flurry of activity occurred within the regional airline industry. AMR, which also operates American Airlines, announced that it planned to sell or spin off Eagle. According to AMR's web site, "The American Eagle network is the largest regional airline system in the world, with over 1,800 daily flights to more than 140 cities throughout the United States, Canada, the Bahamas, the Caribbean and Mexico." Industry profits have been hurt by high fuel costs, and airlines are seeking sources of revenue. Employees affected by this potential move, including the pilot's union, fear an independent Eagle would hire lower wage employees and put their jobs at risk.

In a related news story, United announced plans to offer flights between Washington D.C. and nine east coast cities. In concert with their regional partner, Colgan Air, and under the banner of United Express, these Saab SF–340 smaller jet aircraft will service tertiary airports such as Bradford, Pennsylvania, and south to Shenandoah Valley, Virginia. Out west, Frontier Airlines will launch its regional carrier called Lynx Aviation using 74-seat Bombardier turboprop aircraft to service Wichita, South Dakota, and Sioux City, Iowa. Frontier connects thirty-two cities from the Denver International airport as their hub.

Despite the battle for passengers as noted above, six network airlines began the process of trimming their U.S. flight schedules. According to a *USA Today* analysis of flight schedules, major airlines including American, United, Delta, Continental, Northwest, and US Airways reduced available seats by 4.4 percent than the same time last year. For the traveling public, this means full flights and reduced availability and frequency. This translates into seventy-two thousand fewer seats a day in the continental United States.

Landscape on Airline Industry

In his book, *Seeing What's Next*, Clayton Christensen dedicates a chapter to this very topic and provides a predictive view of the airline industry. He recounts the astounding growth this industry experienced from 1990 through 2000 due to metrics such as increases of revenue-generating customers and average load factor. Conversely, his research illustrates the inability of these carriers to generate a consistent profit. One airline, Southwest, changed the rules through point-to-point service and creating a low cost business model. They took advantage of smaller airports where incumbents wouldn't follow and, in effect, had no competition. Once Southwest exhausted the second-tier airports, its next available space was direct competition with main stream airlines.

The conundrum that Southwest faces today is what Christensen labels fight or flight. In most industries, when the incumbent is faced with a low priced competition, the tendency would be to move to valuable customers (or flight). Because all airlines need to cover their fixed costs, they will now fight for these consumers. This action has caused the major airlines to reinvent themselves, or what Christensen calls Airlines within Airlines. United created Ted by following a similar pattern that Southwest devised: similar aircraft and a service dedicated to the discount traveler. The obvious problem is that no matter how they fashion themselves, it's still the same organization and fixed-cost structure.

There seems to be a pattern here: a new entrant starts at the most unattractive position in the marketplace, mainly low cost air travel, and, over time, migrates into mainstream territory. As noted in news reports, air taxis are sprouting up in smaller, third-tier regional airports that compete against the railway or automobiles, or they have no competition.

Consumer's View

What other events are shaping this market? A rising sentiment in the traveling public's mind surrounds rising fares, delays, cancellations, and poor service. This was the topic of a recent Wall Street Journal article titled "When Fliers Avoid the Domestic Route." It appears the challenge domestic carriers have, in addition to offering low fares, requires balancing costs while keeping the flying public reasonably content. When most airlines were struggling with losses, they began the process of pruning services, charging for movies, and selling box meals. If you desired more leg room, they charged you an additional fee to reside in the preferred zone.

Also noted in this same article was the topic of cleanliness. Travelers are fed up with dirty lavatories, seats, and floors. Air France deep cleans their fleet of aircraft every five weeks, and one domestic airline does so once a month. On long-haul flights, the head rest covers, blankets, and pillows are replaced, but this is not so with domestic runs. There is a perception that foreign carriers are keeping the cabin cleaner and the service staff appears friendlier. The latter issue has merit, and a recent Travelocity poll noted that 59 percent of travelers say that domestic flight attendants are less attentive and 63 percent will purposely avoid airlines with rude personnel.

Another headline from December 2007, posted on Marketing Daily's web site, espoused that "Air Travelers increasingly dislike to fly!" The article speaks to delays, pilot shortages, and security issues as top of mind concerns for an increasing number of surveyed fliers. This article noted that the number of travelers from 2002 to 2007 increased 20 percent, or 665 million annually. According to Mintel International, "39% of respondents from the highest-income households—those making $100,000 or more—are most likely to agree that air travel is not fun. Because high-income households are most likely to fly, it should be a grave concern for the airlines that their most coveted customer group is not particularly fond of air travel or appreciative of the value it provides."

Being a frequent traveler on a variety of carriers affords you the opportunity to query both fellow passengers and flight attendants. The prevailing sentiment that both customer and service provider share can be summed up this way: both feel slighted and unfulfilled. What is the root cause?

Assessment

Let's begin with a basic business model. To effectively compete in this industry, an airline must do the following:

1) Provide safe, timely, clean, and friendly service
2) Offer some level of comfort and convenience
3) Meet the prevailing needs (lifestyles) of consumers
4) Provide a unique, or differentiated, experience

Next, we'll consider the business infrastructure to deliver the above mentioned value proposition. As Clayton Christensen has stated, every company is valued based on three rigors: RPV (resources, process, and value or investments).

Resources

On a daily basis, every airline has the opportunity to garner resources: ability to acquire capital, human assets, and equipment. Not to oversimplify this situation, but all organizations must effectively manage this portion of the equation to be considered a viable player. As a senior member of management, you are readily aware of your financial situation during your monthly meetings with the board.

As noted in the previous section, Southwest Airlines took the opportunity to carve out a segment of the market by targeting the discount traveler. In addition to items one and two, they focused on a segment that was not being readily addressed by the market. They took a novel approach to the market by building a low-cost business structure to match the opportunity. Interestingly, during the same time in the 1980s, Peoples Express and others attempted to follow the discount airline path with high operating costs. This strategy, ultimately, destroyed them.

Let's say your airline followed Southwest's lead and only purchased one aircraft type, utilized point-to-point service, and cross-functionally trained employees. You have a very efficient cost structure with minimal waste, and your organization runs lean. Jet Blue started down this path, but changed directions in favor of high growth and mounting costs.

Process

The process by which you solve daily problems can, in and of itself, destroy an organization. A good example is your business system. If you are upgrading your system and the proper training is absent, this single event could cause a myriad of problems including late flights, duplicate transactions, and inaccurate processing of tickets. The net result of inadequate training prior to a system launch can throw your organization into chaos.

Another green field to consider is management style and approach. If your management applies heavy-handed tactics to accomplish daily routines, the outcome will be felt by internal and external customers alike. A great example might be boardroom edicts that are perception-based and not anchored in the realities of the current situation. For example, let's say your sourcing group recommends local purchases of fuel versus national contracts. Because only senior managers have experience in annual contracts with nationally recognized firms, they dismiss this suggestion. In reality, local suppliers provide a lower total cost—not price-based—because they lack the huge infrastructure and transportation expenses. This disconnect not only reduces operating margins, but it also, in turn, frustrates the employees that are trying to deliver real value back to the organization.

As suggested by Christensen, the process by which employees solve daily problems helps to determine its value. Because your employees live the pain each and every day, they know what works and what doesn't. They are your greatest ally when it comes to efficiency and effectiveness. Some companies recognize this and actually create incentives to effect behavior. Sharing the cost savings with your employees can yield profitable results.

Value

The value or investments made by organizations will help to determine its future net worth. Training programs that increase productivity and promote sound decision making are just a few examples of investments organizations may choose to undertake. The key issues come down to timing: the right program or project at the most appropriate time. For example, switching from manual paperwork for aircraft maintenance to hand-held PDAs not only eliminates redundant information entry, but also enables real-time data on the health of the fleet. Because all organizations have limited time, money, and resources, it's the allocation and effectiveness of these choices that drives organizational value.

Summation of findings

Using the four value criteria noted above and factoring in RPV, you've come to the following conclusions about your business model: First, providing safe, timely, and friendly service is a baseline requirement for entry into this market. Your new fleet of small aircraft, lean and efficient systems, and process enable a high percentage of on-time arrivals. In addition, your staff embrace a "customer first" approach that has been embedded into your culture. So far, so good!

Second, the investments you've made provide reasonably comfortable seating, clean cabins and surroundings, and convenient and easy to use on-line reservations. Next, you are in-step with the prevailing lifestyles of the market segment you're serving. Although business travelers may choose your airline on occasion, your "meat and potato" business resides in the discounted fare market. Finally, providing a unique experience that is differentiated is critical. This is the heart of your branding strategy.

Value Gap Analysis

It seems rather clear that running a profitable airline business in today's environment has its challenges. Now that you have determined the correct business model, let's turn our attention to gaps in the marketplace. The essence of a value gap analysis is to establish the primary attributes that are important to customers. You may develop one profile for the discount traveler and another that addresses the business segment. Two critical areas should be noted here: the method of data collection and adaptation to your business model.

Surveys and other polling methods may only scratch the surface when it comes to understanding human behavior. As consumers, we have a tendency to fib when asked about our opinion. As Tom Kelly noted in his book *The Art of Innovation*, "your customers may lack the vocabulary or the palate to explain what's wrong, and especially what's missing." For a multitude of reasons, our responses do not reflect our true nature. A more meaningful approach to understanding how consumers use our products or services is simply to observe behavior.

As a progressive and out-of-the-box thinker, you decide to take this method to heart and hire several observers who are skilled at observation and data collection. Next, you rotate them through your different routes and markets as well as three top competitors. One group focuses on the discount traveler and the other on the business segment. They are all approachable, friendly, and attentive. Their primary job is to listen to travelers and understand how they use this service. On a daily basis, they log their observations, frustrations, and the temperament of the two groups. Over time, this data will reflect patterns of use and common opinions. The observer will attempt to objectively rank these impressions by importance and value to the traveler.

Based on the findings above, you construct a value-gap radar graph to evaluate your discount travelers. You segregate the key attributes that this group ranked as most important and settle on five to seven aspects that determine a pleasant experience. These attributes include food, friendly service, comfort, on-time arrivals and departures, and frequency of service. Discount travelers commented on experiences with three other airlines (AL) on these specific attributes. This information is corroborated by survey kiosks placed in boarding areas.

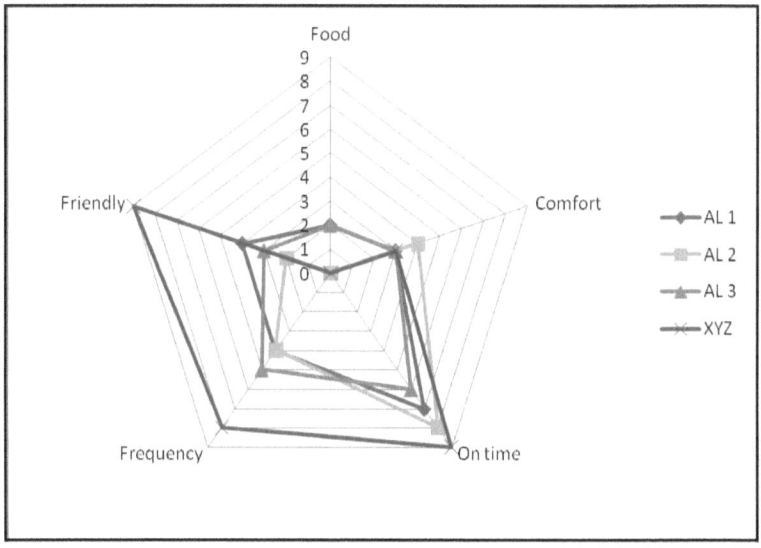

For this group, food and comfortable seating were less valued, probably as a result of the short duration of the flight. The most important aspect was on-time arrivals and departures. All airlines were ranked closely in this regard. An obvious gap appears on the radar for frequency of flights and friendly service. For the discount traveler, a point of differentiation has emerged. Let's turn our attention to the more prized business traveling segment.

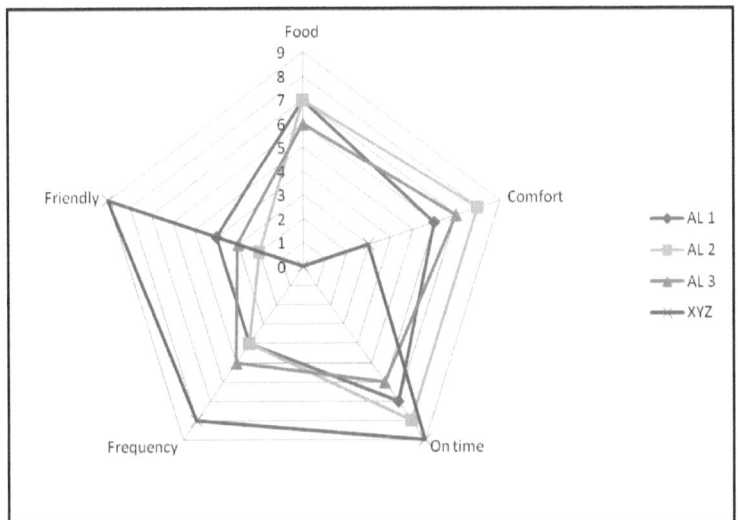

As you can see, the type of service expected from the business traveler varies and requires a different set of attributes. In addition to on-time delivery, these travelers desire food and comfort as part of their experience. Despite the fact that frequency of flights and attentive personnel were ranked less, this group valued the perks, such as premium seating, and food options on flights greater than two hours. The obvious gap that exists for XYZ naturally occurs in this region.

As further noted in Tom Kelly's book, an obvious cornerstone of IDEO's (Palo Alto based Design Firm) success formula is Innovation Begins with an Eye! He quickly espouses that IDEO products were inspired by watching real people in real settings, not a focus group. Kelly suggests that "seeing and hearing things with your own eyes and ears is a critical first step in improving or creating a breakthrough product." He goes on to say that "many entrepreneurs got started by observing humans struggle with tired routines and started asking themselves what they could do about it."

Kelly points out an inherent challenge with the survey process. First, people are too polite to really tell you what they think. As he suggests, if you ask how the food tasted, they will simply provide the kind of feedback they believe you are seeking. Second, your customers don't possess the vocabulary to tell you what they want. If you ask a Sony CD player user to comment on the next revolution in mobile music, his or her only reference will be the current technology, and responses will center on incremental improvements. Conversely, if you observe the struggles users have with the technology, opportunities for improvements will abound.

Brand Triad Model Applied

With observation data in hand, you are ready to apply the brand triad model. Let's begin with the A–B relationship. The attributes of your offering, service, and the behavior of your consumers, desire, determine how you deliver value. Through continual solicitation and observation, you uncover *how* consumers use your service and *why*. This may seem rudimentary to most executives, but understanding the purpose or fundamental use for a given product or service is less understood than most care to admit.

Whether you're on a business trip or a much needed vacation, most of us choose to fly as a means to reach our destination in an expeditious manner.

The attributes of XYZ Airline include

- Functional attributes:
    - o   Recognized brand
    - o   Well-run
    - o   New aircraft
    - o   Convenient departure times and destinations
    - o   Affordable
- Emotional attributes:
    - o   Safe and reliable
    - o   Clean, bright, and inviting aircraft

o   Entertaining: light-hearted crew relieves stress of flying

o   Comforting: employees make you feel important and comfortable

The behavioral aspects include

- Functional:

  o   Departure airports are conveniently located

  o   Traveling needs are suitable

  o   Web-based reservations provide a wide array of choices (control)

  o   Last minute flights are easy to catch (freedom)

  o   No fees for exchanging tickets (hassle-free)

- Emotional:

  o   Consistent value (what you see is what you get)

  o   Luxurious: cabin seats are leather

  o   Calming: interior colors are cool shades

  o   Relaxing: music before departure is tranquil

As previously discussed, striking a balance between the attributes of your offering and the desire (behaviors) of the traveling public will determine your level of success with your target audience. Using surveys and observing fellow passengers, develop a scattering of opinions and rank them on the scale. If your collective offering matches the flying public's current needs, then the results should closely align near the zero point on the continuum.

If you are the average traveling consumer, the attributes of frequent, friendly, and on-time service fits with both the observation and survey kiosk data. XYZs model works well here, and a clear gap exists for further discount traveler segment exploitation. However, when considering the business segment data, amenities such as food and comfort are the preferred choice. Despite the fact that the most sought after business segment will choose XYZ in a pinch (reliable travel alternative), the attributes of the offering are not a good fit.

As a result, the plot point on our A–B graph moves toward desire (behaviors) and away from attributes for the business traveler. This occurs naturally because people will modify their behavior (away from zero, or core offering) and accept an affiliate option. However, if this segment becomes a strategic initiative in the future, adding a small business section (similar to most regional jets) might be your next move. What important insight was gleaned from this A–B analysis? It clarifies your current state and forces the management team to rethink their future strategy.

As with any strategic move, there are risks and consequences. If you alter your winning strategy by shifting toward the business traveler, you now open the door to new opportunities as well as competition. The resources available to you will now be divided between offensive and defensive tactics that might dilute other internal initiatives. As with any war, opening up a new front requires the deployment of scarce resources. The question that management should consider is will the incremental revenue and margin increase, in the long run, exceed the cost to the current operations?

The next assessment will consist of behavior as it relates to the circumstance of air travel. We already determined the behavior associated with flying XYZ, but now we will compare that to the circumstances in which consumers fly:

- Functional Circumstances:
    o Web-based reservations system
    o Local airport
    o Accessible parking
    o Quick processing through ticketing and security
    o Accessible shops and restaurants in terminal
    o Fast boarding on flight
    o No delays
    o Expeditious baggage processing
- Emotional Circumstances:
    o Good experience from start to finish
    o Friendly service
    o Good feelings
    o Nice surroundings

As previously discussed, we all try to achieve a convenient and enjoyable set of circumstances when we engage brands. Based on circumstances, the functional aspects of engaging the traveling public come down to convenience. From start to finish, the consumer seeks the path of least resistance when it comes to flying. This process starts with the most convenient and least congested airport that offers the amenities which suit a given scenario. As noted in one *Wall Street Journal* article (Dec. 2007), consumers are willing to drive long distances to avoid unattractive experiences with major airports. Conversely, when traveling on business or abroad, your choices (circumstances) may be limited and, thus, force a move from an optimal scenario to one of a less desirable affiliate or periphery choice.

Shift from Theory to Personal Experience

Recently, I had the option of flying from Orange County to San Francisco. The circumstances surrounding my choice came down to three airports: San Francisco International, San Jose, and Oakland. From prior experience, San Francisco International can be challenging if weather (fog, rain, etc) is present, thereby shutting down one runway and leading to delays and cancellations. On the other hand, it is a short cab ride to the city, and the airport offers many amenities sought during layovers: restaurants, bookstores, and displays. San Jose, on the other hand, is the farthest option available and a very expensive cab fare to the city. Conversely, this airport is smaller, easy to get in and out of, and convenient for business in the South Bay. My only logical choice is Oakland. Because my personal preference is San Francisco International (core brand) followed by San Jose (affiliate), I am forced to select a periphery offering (Oakland).

This mental exercise plays in the minds of consumers on a daily basis. Consumers all try to strike a balance between preferences (behavior) and prevailing circumstances. Without understanding this process or the struggles the traveling public faces, we can't possibly understand how consumers use our products or services. The concept of employing observers on flights can begin the process of mapping the circumstances from start to finish as they relate to behavior (B–C). The insight obtained from this exercise far outweighs any quantitative survey results.

The last comparison sets attributes against circumstances. Because we already defined both, let's simply draw a summary of our known findings.

Circumstances are Key

As previously mentioned, the attributes of your product or service as they relate to the prevailing circumstances demonstrate how far consumers will go to select a core brand. A good example comes in the form of frequent flier programs. Being a United Premier Executive affords me many advantages that are not readily available to the lion's share of the traveling public. United recently installed a Premier Zone with extra legroom near the front of each cabin. In addition, they allow this class of traveler's priority during the boarding process. After completing a series of segments, the program grants free electronic upgrades that can be requested during the online booking stage of a given ticket purchase. The attributes of the United Airline brand (as with other airlines) incentivize business travelers to make that airline their desired core brand. As a long-time user of this service, my natural inclination leads me to consider their offering first before moving on to more affordable and direct options. Only after exhausting every possible option (route and price) available with United will I switch to another carrier. This is especially true when it comes to international flights where frequent flier mileage translates into a business class upgrade.

Once the attributes are assessed and deemed favorable, the circumstances side of the equation comes into play. Despite the fact that we have settled on favorable attributes, the circumstances of use may fail our expectations. What does this mean? An event may occur before the flight, during, or upon reaching the destination. In the process of traveling with a given brand, a breakdown in the process (steps-to-execution) may evolve and, in extreme cases, lead to a disconnect. These may include lost baggage, double booking a seat, a dirty bathroom, flight delays, and a myriad of other events just to name a few.

When selecting a future flight, and based on the above mentioned issues, the traveling public seeks a balance between the attributes of a given brand (airline) and the circumstances in which they travel. After taking all things into consideration, any movement from the zero location on the A–C continuum may shift based on the prevailing events (both operational and environmental). If XYZ Airline develops a reputation for flight delays due to organizational dysfunction, the natural inclination on the part of the traveling public will be to mentally shift the brand perception from core to affiliate or periphery category. The movement will be away from attributes and toward circumstances.

Conversely, if the attributes are functioning in comparison to similar competitors but the circumstances surrounding its use fails, then the point moves away from circumstances and shifts to other offerings. Movement away from equilibrium indicates consumers are adjusting to the prevailing situation. In essence, they are either changing carriers (attributes) or modifying their normal routines (circumstances) to achieve a level of satisfaction.

Summation of Findings

The scatter matrix below represents a compilation of all three aspects of the brand triad for both the discount and business traveler scenarios. As illustrated, XYZ Airlines has a tight scatter around plot point zero for the discount traveler model. The significance of these findings both supports and acknowledges that they are well positioned for the audience they serve, and they possess the right combination of attributes for future growth. The radar model demonstrates a distinct gap between XYZ and other airlines and, thus, demonstrates room for market acquisition or growth. If XYZ stays true to their value proposition, they could be perceived as the new "low cost model" and potentially usurp those that have moved up market, such as Southwest Airlines. Capitalizing on this gap may include a gradual expansion into secondary and tertiary airports where other low cost incumbents reside.

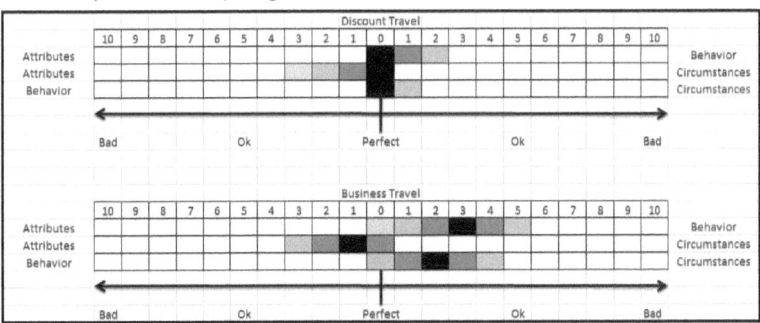

Conversely, the scattergram indicates that XYZ is not well positioned for the business traveler segment. These business travelers are willing to trade frequency of flights and a less friendly staff for other amenities such as food and comfort. Based on first-person observations combined with kiosk surveys, the resultant business traveler must modify his or her behavior (desire for business class amenities) when selecting XYZ Airlines.

Triad Relationship

If you were to assemble the three legs together to form an equilateral triangle, one can quickly see the alignments and offsets of your brand for a given target audience. In the case of discount travelers, all three legs have scatter data tightly surrounding the mid-point (zero location). In a perfect world, all three segments would be nicely centered near zero on each continuum. The beauty of this exercise is to assess the distance from zero and what direction the company should to move to achieve balance. By benchmarking your current position, the management team can begin the process of weighing the costs associated with a shift in direction.

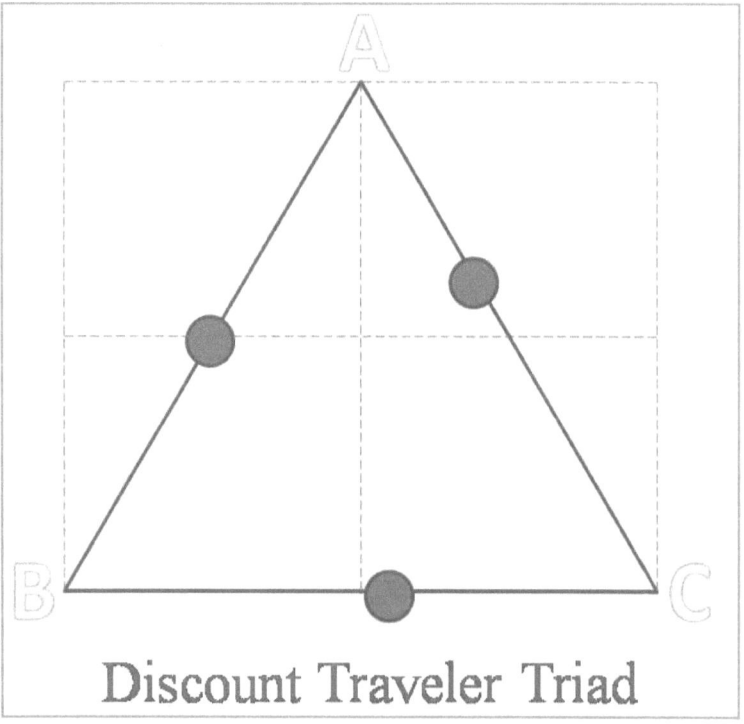

Discount Traveler Triad

With respect to the business traveling segment, the offsets between the three continuums are more pronounced and clearly indicate that the current XYZ platform is not well suited to address the needs of this marketplace.

Upon further investigation, it's clear that the attributes to behavior relationship demonstrates the extent business travelers must modify their actions to accommodate the XYZ offering. The further the distance from attributes, the less suitable a product or service becomes.

A good example is Sony and their Walkman product. During the 1990s, and with no other equivalent offering in the marketplace, Sony's CD player was viewed by the buying public as "good enough," or the staple product of choice. When the iPod came on the scene, early adopters, always seeking a better solution, viewed the new offering as a better fit with their behavior (needs and desires) and shifted away from the CD attributes. A scattergram on customer behavior would have signaled this phenomenon was underway. It's clear that Sony's management was unaware of this shift .).

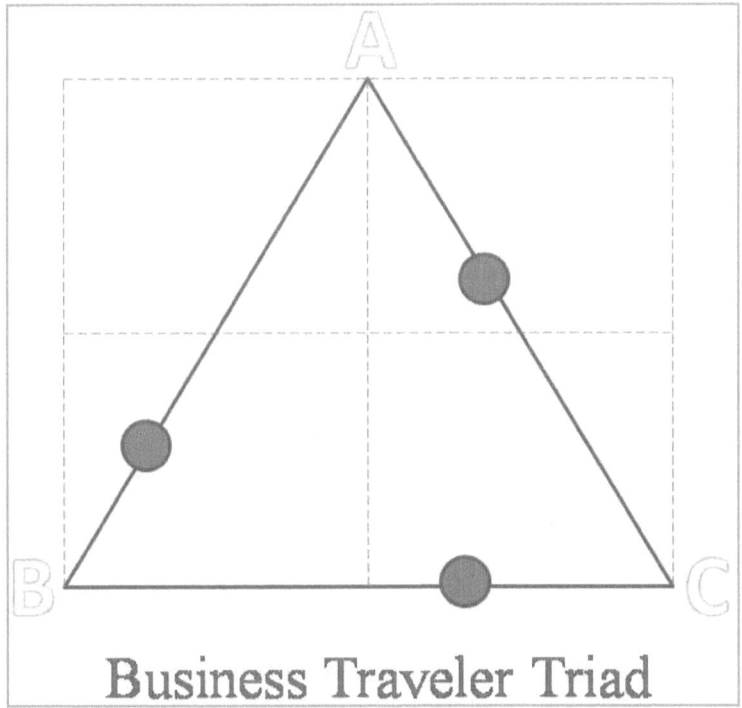

Business Traveler Triad

Once a disruption emerges that requires little effort to change, compared to the enormous benefit acquired, an almost viral awaking of ideas occurs in the marketplace that creates a tsunami of behavioral change. If one were to follow the Sony demise to its natural conclusion, the plot point would continue to shift away from attributes and eventually fall off the continuum itself because consumers stop purchasing. What similarities can we draw between the Sony example and our analysis of XYZ Airline?

A Common Thread

The idea of mobile music and air travel can be viewed as the denominator if one were to think in terms of a fraction (ex. Walkman/ mobile music). In both cases, the concept of mobile music and air travel hasn't changed over time. Whether an 8-track player, cassette tape, CD, or iPod, we have come to expect and appreciate our ability to carry our music with us, albeit in a variety of forms big and small. So the idea of mobile music isn't new: it's the packaging or delivery vehicle that has improved and become more user-friendly (the numerator). The iPod's small size, shuffle or random access, connectivity through your computer, iTunes music store (instant downloads), and hip design provide an enormous gain over inserting large CDs into a bulky, awkward, and hard to handle player. Case closed!

Air travel is no different: Southwest clearly did the same thing. The denominator in the fractional equation of air travel (aircraft, reservation systems, amenities, personnel, other attributes) was roughly equal. At any given time, other airlines could have created a scattergram by observing behavior and then noted a shift in use. These airlines could have witnessed the signals of change and started a separate operation (new offering) and applied a similar approach (low cost model).

Unfortunately, they allowed a seemingly insignificant regional airline (disruptor) to germinate and grow into the new standard (like iPod) for domestic travel. As a result, other carriers were forced to followed suit and morphed into a similar offering to defend their base business. The question remains: how well do they match the Southwest brand, and will consumers view them as authentic or a duplicate?

As previously mentioned, XYZ is disadvantaged when it comes to the business traveler segment. Although they share in a portion of this business through reluctant users, the question management must address is what incremental benefit will they achieve versus the cost to alter their successful business model (both financial and brand equity)? As the vice president of marketing for XYZ Airline, this is the tough question you must answer.

Nano Branding

Another aspect that XYZ Airlines may want to consider is how deep is your relationship with your customers? Whether it's the discount or business traveler segment, both possess additional information and analysis that may help to uncover the current state of your customer base and possible signals as to future preferences. As we learned in the mobile music field, changing the delivery vehicle can have a profound impact on the state of an industry.

A prior chapter dealt with the application of continuums of the brand triad. As previously discussed, each leg has a second dimension (vertical) which depicts the level of satisfaction or brand engagement.

This measurement tool could help management understand the depth to which their current users are connected to their brand offering. Why is this important? Before a company witnesses a shift on the main continuum, a more subtle movement occurs on this secondary (vertical) continuum that speaks to how engaged your audience has become.

Imagine you stay at the same hotel for business purposes an average of four days per month. For this example, let's suggest your main continuums are all in balance: you are reasonably satisfied and all plot points are near zero. Despite the fact that all your needs are met, you are not engaged with the current hotel brand. As the consumer, it's good enough and you've built a habit around this activity. If we were to measure your connectivity to this hotel brand, it might be a three on a scale of ten. In short, anything less than a five would be considered mild indifference towards a brand.

On your next trip, you notice a new hotel nearby that appears more attractive (outward aesthetics), so you inquire with your associates who reside in the area. They, in turn, offer their opinions and experiences (viral), and this information would be viewed as a credible source. If one were to measure your brand connectivity with the current hotel brand, it would naturally begin to drop. Why would this happen?

As consumers, we are constantly assessing our options and weighing them against current offerings. If we stumble across a new brand, we are naturally skeptical and curious at the same time. With the hotel example, we view this opportunity as a way to increase our experience (desire) for roughly the same expenditure. As a result, our business traveler may book a room to test out these assumptions and determine if they are indeed correct. During the stay, our business traveler discovers more pleasing amenities and services not offered elsewhere, and the connectivity toward the current brand erodes even further.

To borrow a contemporary business phrase, the tipping point has been achieved. Without any intervention by the current hotel, the subtle movement along the connectivity continuum has dropped further and has made this brand indistinguishable. The natural progression has begun and jumps to the attributes–behavior continuum. As the new hotel moves from casual to preferred use, the plot point of the current hotel moves away from attributes and toward behavior. If the new hotel offers on-line amenities during the reservation process, the relationship between the user and new offering grows deeper. At some point when the business traveler makes a permanent switch to the new hotel, the plot point falls off the main continuum (for the old hotel). The other aspects of the triad, namely A–C and B–C remain relatively constant for both hotels because those aspects have no bearing on the situation.

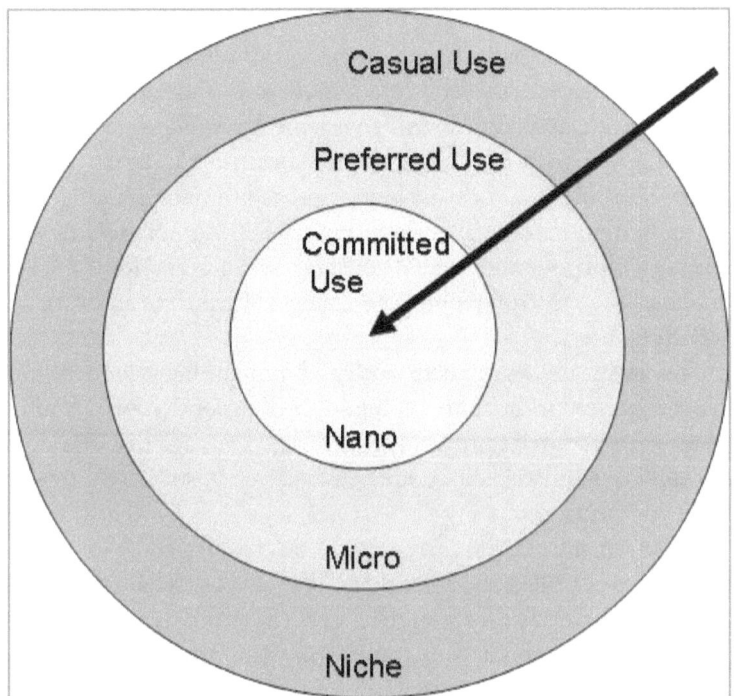

The importance of monitoring the more subtle movements in consumer behavior (engagement) may act as an early warning signal for your business. These activities occur over time and are not some sudden event. Consumers need time to process new attributes, behaviors, and circumstances for each new brand. Whether your business is air travel, mobile music, or hotels, consumers are constantly searching the marketplace of ideas to help provide solutions to their daily struggles.

Outcomes

The challenge for the vice president of marketing at this juncture is to step back from the situation and review the different options (business strategy) available to XYZ Airlines. Based on the observations and survey data, the most attractive market segment for XYZ to pursue is the discount traveler. Because the bench strength of the organization (core business) was built around low cost operation and serving the nonbusiness user, it seems reasonable to leverage the strengths of the core and attack those secondary and tertiary markets.

The outcome of this assessment means XYZ continues to invest in activities that strengthen their core offering and invest in penetrating adjacent markets. In addition, they continue to monitor the more subtle aspects of brand engagement to understand the level of connectivity with their constituency. Because consumer behavior is in constant motion, a closed-loop approach to understanding these nuances is important. A closed-loop approach is another way of staying connected with your audience. A constant outreach and feedback loop will allow XYZ to truly appreciate changes within the industry and reactions by users.

The use of surveys can help track and monitor behavior over time. This doesn't need to be some boring piece of paper that you hand out as consumers board the aircraft. I recall several years ago that one airline gave mileage points if you completed a survey. Also, I have received e-mails inquiring about my stay several days after staying in certain hotels. How many of these surveys have you completed? I can honestly say that I haven't filled in one of them. Why does this happen?

As the marketing vice president of XYZ, you may want to think more innovatively about your cause, and place yourself in the shoes of your audience. Consumers lives are busy enough, and they don't have time to burn by helping out a business with their market research project. The perception might be that the airline or hotel company already has our money (pay for play) and giving any more time actually costs us (as consumers). In effect, you are asking consumers to pay again.

As previously mentioned, use the time when consumers are readily open and available to you to seek understanding and find new, creative ways to uncover their needs. The opportune time comes when consumers are seeking *you* through *your* on-line reservation session. You can accomplish their objectives (booking a flight or hotel stay) and learn about their behaviors at the same time. Be careful: there is a delicate balance between taking care of their needs while gently gathering information about consumer preferences—iTunes does this by suggesting similar genre songs as voted by fellow iPoders.

Consider this: When consumers are seeking you out (for information, products, services, etc.) they are in a buying mode. When you approach them (advertising, spam, etc.), you are in a selling mode. Consumers love to buy on their time schedule and terms. While they are booking, treat them with great care and concern. I don't know a single person who doesn't enjoy VIP treatment. During the process, gently ask them about other amenities that might make their flight or hotel stay more pleasurable. Once they take interest by responding, make sure your web page reacts quickly: reduce flash and other hard to load graphics and give them the information they seek. Take this information and add it to their profile. If you have an intelligent system (like Amazon or iTunes), you can present new layers of information or recommendations to enhance their travel needs. By constantly digging deeper into consumers preferences, the better you can serve their needs. On the connectivity scale, each new engagement increases your brand value in the mind's eye of the consumer's. They indeed move from being a casual to a committed user.

The latter discussion dealt with the discount traveler, but what about the more profitable business segment? There is no doubt that any airline can gain greater margins for the same flight by populating a percentage of their seats with high-ticket-priced travelers. The analysis required to assess the incremental gain by adopting this strategy goes far beyond the scope of this book. That is clearly a job for each company to analyze from sales to operations, and it includes a detailed look at the market space. What this book offers is a visual recognition that either an opportunity or threat exists and offers help to the organization planning for a change in direction. That said, this chapter closes by viewing the triad model once again and focusing on the two options and future direction available to XYZ.

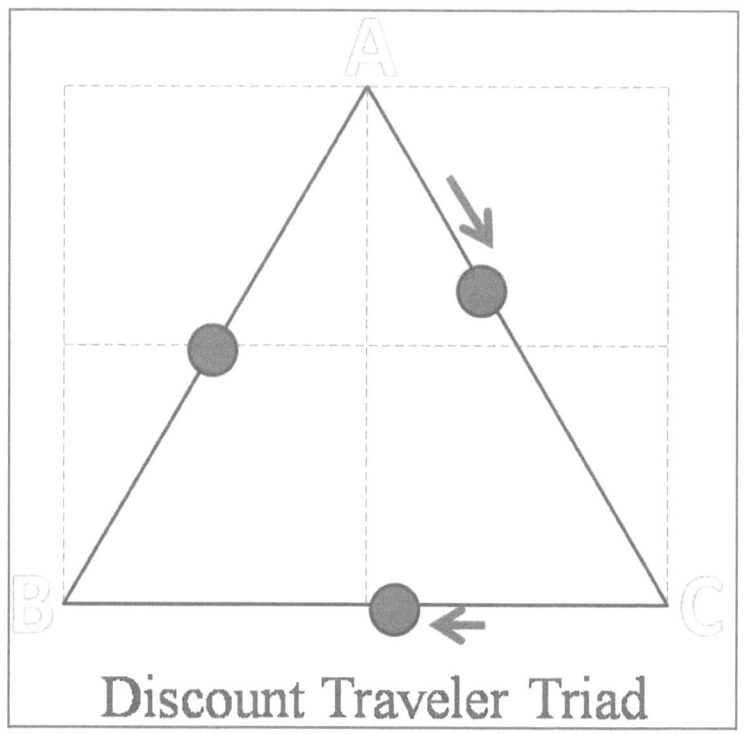

Discount Traveler Triad

Options Based on Triad Findings

A review of our triad model for the discount segment is by far the easier of the two options because the offsets (distance) from all equilibriums are relatively small. Going back to the radar graph, one could dig deeper into both the observation and survey data to uncover specifics surrounding both the A–C and B–C events. In some cases, the ability to change attributes to circumstances goes beyond the control of business and is, therefore, the same for all competitors. This might include long Transportation Security Administration (TSA) lines or wait time to unload and deliver baggage to the carousel. The real value of this exercise unveils what you can and can't control and how that impacts your brand. Without understanding these more granular details, a business could miss the subtle differences that distinguish one business from another and, thus, contribute to brand erosion.

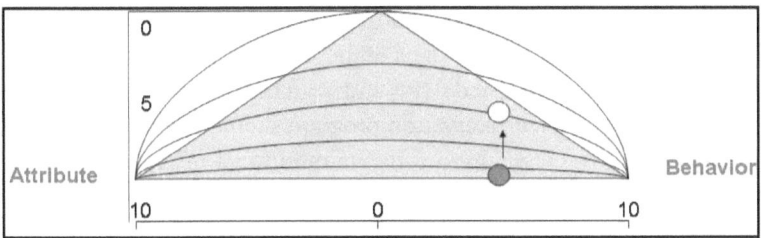

A more challenging but doable study would be to assess how connected (engaged) your customers are at any given time. The previously noted hotel example demonstrated this process. A consumer can employ a product or service out of habit, but the level of brand engagement may be lacking. This consumer could be ripe for the picking by the competition. The closer to the zero point on the connectivity graph, the more susceptible they are to switching brands. How do you gauge this more elusive measurement?

There are several ways to approach measurement on a second dimension. Traditional surveys and kiosks could garner a broad understanding of brand connectivity. You can also monitor your web traffic by using a free tool called Google Analytics, which provides detailed information in a Dash Board setting. Here you can understand visitors, traffic sources, page views, time on site, and loyalty (return visits). This provides a profile of how visitors are using your site and the path they take once they arrive (landing and exit pages). A more targeted and meaningful way of collecting valuable data goes back to the point of engagement. By tracking return visits to a registered profile, you can start to assess loyalty to your offering. The more frequent the return visits, the more connected your customer base has become. Let me provide an example.

Being a United Premier Executive affords me preferential seating on most flights booked. Recently, I began a search for an upcoming European trip and naturally started with United. Having made this trip several times, I was very familiar with the type of aircraft deployed and amenities associated with them. For me, a comfortable seat and personal entertainment controls are high on my list. Despite my many attempts (routings in various cities), the time frame or equipment (older aircraft) did not suit my needs and, as a result, I started looking at competing offerings.

Based on the aircraft type and associated amenities, I eventually settled on a foreign carrier that I've never tried before. The point is that I went back to United's site and searched the same destination several times, and their reservation program should have taken note of this activity. If the reservation software monitored my many attempts to book a flight to London, it would have suggested alternatives, or an actual sales representative should have intervened and attempted to solve my dilemma. By not addressing this subtle event, my last three trips to Europe have been with alternate carriers, and United has indeed lost this valuable income stream. In short, subtlety counts!

A recent *Wall Street Journal* article actually addressed this very issue and suggested technology tools could improve customer experience. These tools include measurement, tracking, and monitoring customer experience. As noted in the article, U.S. Airways utilized software called TeaLeaf Technology, which allowed airline employees to "replay and review screen shots of the web site when customers encountered a problem." By fixing the problem, those that encountered ticket purchasing problems achieved 100 percent completion of their order processing. Another program, by Microsoft Corp.'s Avenue A/Razorfish, helps to understand customer behavior and realign web strategy. The article went on to state that Forrester and Shop.org research indicates online retailers will increase spending on customer retention initiatives in 2008. "Many companies realize that consumers making transactions on their web sites are a mouse-click away from patronizing a rival." Touché.

Business Segment

Let's now look at our business traveler option. As noted above, a smaller movement along the A–C continuum may be partially related to changes in operations or uncontrollable events such as airport security. The B–C continuum may require greater investigation because you are now delving into changing behavior. Finally, to move toward attributes requires a fundamental change in XYZs offering. As previously mentioned, this shift would demand much more than adding business seating and altering the web site. This shift requires both a business and brand shift (reorganization) that may affect future rules of engagement and alter the landscape of this market.

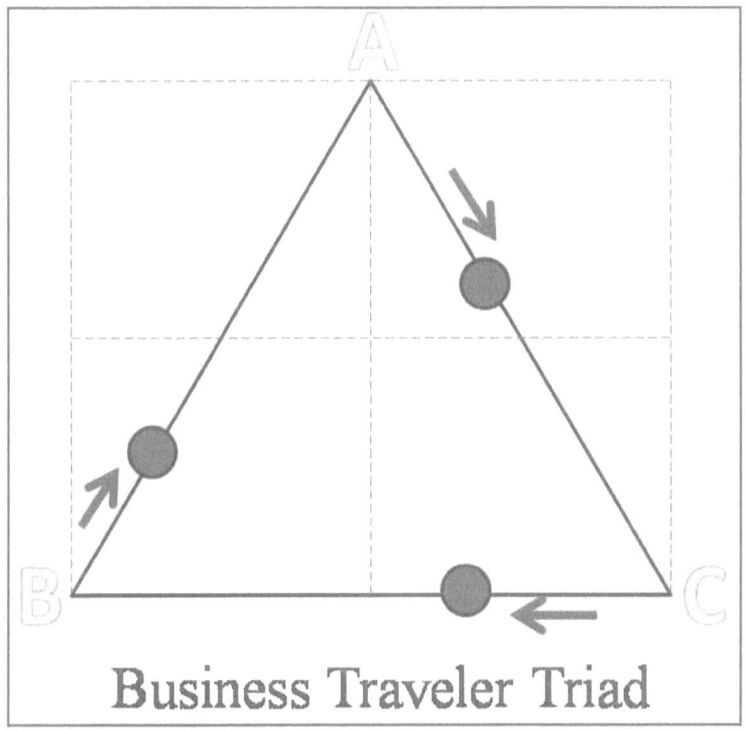

Business Traveler Triad

If XYZ Airlines chooses this path, the importance of monitoring the second dimension becomes even more critical. Noting subtle changes in consumer perception will provide advance warning of shifts along any of the three continuums. A novel approach to actively communicate with patrons is to create both a blog and discussion forum on the company web site. Select someone in your organization as the designated blogger. Over time, this voice will be viewed as authentic and can speak to this community about their concerns and questions, and he or she can allow them to air their opinions. For example, a national news circuit, CNN, reported the following regarding Southwest Airlines and allegations surrounding their maintenance compliance:

Southwest Airlines tried to keep serious problems with its maintenance program hidden and pressured the Federal Aviation Administration to keep out an inspector who noticed the problems, according to two FAA inspectors who blew the whistle on the airline.

In turn, Southwest's blog responded accordingly:

WE TAKE SAFETY SERIOUSLY
By: Paula Berg - Southwest Airlines

Friends—Many of you are writing to us concerned about today's news reports regarding the safety and inspections of Southwest Airlines' aircraft.

Let me assure you, first and foremost, that no one is more passionate about the safety of our Customers and Employees than we are, and it is important for you all to know that the situation being reported in the media was never and is not now a safety of flight issue.

The FAA has issued what is called a "letter of penalty" to Southwest Airlines regarding one of many routine, redundant, and overlapping inspections of our fleet. The specific inspection in question involves an extremely small area in one of many overlapping inspections designed to detect early signs of skin cracking on our aircraft.

In March 2007, Southwest Airlines discovered a missed inspection area, disclosed the information to the FAA, and promptly re-inspected all of our potentially affected aircraft.

The FAA approved our actions at that time and considered the matter closed as of April 2007.

(Used with Permisision)

What followed was a frank and open conversation by participants ranging from patrons to airline pilots and everyone in between. The following dialogue is a sample from the blog roll of Southwest Airlines:

Good work SWA…meeting the problem head on. You'll still see me onboard!

Posted by: | March 11, 2008 at 3:34 pm

I have been regularly flying SWA for 12 years, more than 50 round trips a year.

I regret to see SWA being in this situation. Some of the management needs to be fired too because they took their job for granted.

It can't be merely confined to just a few employees. So let us see some action where some people get fired & prison time.

Posted by: | March 11, 2008 at 3:37 pm

I am truly disappointed and will not fly with SWA anymore! The company is still in denial of its wrong doing. Small cracks will turn into large, dangerous ones without prompt repairs. Stop lying and doing superficial change. It's time for real top-down reform.

Posted by: | March 11, 2008 at 4:10 pm

You're being dramatic. Commercial Airplanes are purposefully over-engineered. I'd rather have the employees (and let us not forget that managers are still people and employees) who has gone through this and made the screwup, been publicly called on the carpet still in the seat. Why? There is no way they'll do it again.

Posted by:| March 11, 2008 at 4:49 pm

(Used with Permission)

In addition to the airline's web site, monitoring blogs and social network forums such as YouTube will help keep the company's ear to the ground on relevant events. The key point here is that the rules of one-way communication are gone forever. With the advent of the Internet, blogs, discussion boards, and self-created web sites, the ability for the masses to voice their opinion is ever present. Sticking your head in the sand on current issues, especially well known brands, can be disastrous. Consider what happened to Firestone concerning tires and SUVs. Although one could attribute the problem as being more PR related (silence versus confronting the issue in the media), allowing your audience a forum to vent their concerns is critical.

This court of appeals enables a democratic approach to dealing with issues through a healthy debate. Thought leaders can chime in and help keep the facts intact. By allowing your constituency to vent and debate the issue, coupled with direct dialogue by a company spokesperson, you can turn a PR nightmare into constructive conversation. In the end, people want to know that big business, and small business too, are listening and correcting the wrong. Management needs to stop hiding behind scripted press releases and invest in an open and honest dialogue with consumers.

XYZ has much to think about when it comes to selecting a strategic direction for the future. The investigation process undertaken helped to uncover the current state of business and assess XYZs position within the industry. Next, we distilled many key aspects that travelers deemed important for both segments. This was accomplished by surveying the target audience (discount travelers) and a potential growth segment (business). In addition, a small group of observers were employed to witness the actual behavior of the collective group. This process included XYZ and its three closest competitors. In this manner, a reliable scatter of data could be garnered that focused on important matters in the mind's eye of these two segments.

Once the data was collected and analyzed, the next step was to undertake a value gap analysis and overlay this information onto a radar chart. This pictorial provided a first look at the differences between offerings based on key aspects, the competition, and survey results for both segments. This critical analysis generated insight into two important areas: differences and similarities in the competitive landscape and existing gaps that are not being readily addressed.

You're Toolbox: Value Gap Analysis and Scattergram

Many years ago, I attended a lecture series at Oxford University, and one presenter, Dr. Richard Schoenberg, illustrated why some organizations succeed while others fail to harness the essence of customer satisfaction. His concept could be applied to any ongoing concern and quickly depicts gaps between products and services offered and actual consumer behavior.

The framework of a value gap analysis is comprised of two constituencies: identification of gaps in consumer value that are not being fulfilled and redefining the competitive rules. In the 1980s, Southwest Airlines found a gap—low-cost, no frills travel—in the airline industry and built a business model around that unfulfilled need. Management understood that competing head-to-head, using the rules of the other giant airlines, meant certain disaster. Southwest Airlines, in effect, changed the rules and was rewarded with market dominance and monetary prosperity during tumultuous times. Southwest built a low-cost business model by employing point-to-point service; utilizing one aircraft type (Boeing 737), which reduced maintenance costs; and cross-functionally trained all their employees.

A value gap analysis consists of plotting your direct competitors on at least seven key attributes they consistently deliver. Next, by observing behavior or collecting surveys, your target audience rates each attribute in terms of importance. The variance between competitive offerings and customer behavior will readily emerge. By reducing, eliminating, or increasing those attributes, a new position will be created that more accurately suits the behavior of your targeted audience. This exercise not only identifies opportunities, but it also reduces or eliminates activities that consumers do not value and, in turn, reduces associated costs.

If we apply this concept to the Southwest example, one can quickly assimilate attributes of importance to the discount traveler and, by filling those needs, discern how a successful business might be developed. Customers felt that food and comfort, which airlines were offering, possessed little value when compared to on-time flights and a fun experience. As a result, Southwest eliminated meals and minimized seating but focused on frequency of on-time flights and created a fun experience from check-in to the destination arrival. Part of the "fun" included wise-cracks made by flight attendants, group singing, and good-natured humor throughout the flight.

To summarize, Dr. Richard Schoenberg suggests mapping the behavior of your target audience and finding gaps that are being ignored or underdeveloped. Next, adjust your business model to eliminate, reduce, or increase value in areas that are meaningful to the user. Finally, change the rules of the game and make them hard to follow.

The next step involves placing this data onto a scattergram. The scale is predicated on how consumers rank their experiences from best to worst. The scatter data also illustrates the intensity of responses based on color: darker reflects more responses, lighter equals fewer. One could also replace shades of color with a bell curve or vertical bar chart. The important point here is to accurately measure and express the consumer's experience, both positive and negative. The scattergram, as previously demonstrated, helps reflect the concentration of perceptions for any of the three continuums. Once compiled, a distinct plot point will unveil itself for each leg and provide a current state of affairs. Because people and events are in constant motion, this assessment should be constantly monitored to identify shifts that are underway.

The final step is to build a triad model for each of the two market segments and plot all three continuums. This effort will allow senior management the opportunity to assess their current position and quickly determine potential options. In addition, a more subtle second dimension should be closely monitored to understand small changes that eventually lead to large shifts on the main continuum. You may recall that the second dimension is a precursor to major shifts in consumer behavior. The hotel example illustrated how a patron can be lulled into switching brands unless an intervention takes place. The overriding importance of this assessment gives managers a broader and clearer view of their current landscape of business and, at the same time, allows them to see the storm clouds that are gathering on the horizon.

With this completed model in hand, managers can compare and contrast the cost-benefits to driving a shift on any of the three continuums. This may be as simple as a new promotional campaign to highlight certain amenities or as radical as tearing out seats and creating a new business section. Whatever the decision, an in-depth financial analysis must be pursued to truly understand the ramifications of each option. In addition to risk assessment, the addressable market and competitive scenarios must be played out to understand possible outcomes of each decision. Running a simulation on many possible options will help to anticipate and plan for counterattacks that may be required. For more information on this type of scenario planning, you may want to read *Hyper Competition: Managing the Dynamics of Strategic Maneuvering* by Dr. Richard D'Aveni.

One final consideration before you attempt the triad model: As with any decision-making process, our view of the horizon may be clouded or obstructed for a variety of reasons. This may occur because we are so enamored with our idea that we can't see the forest from the trees. A distorted view may be introduced because we seek council from others, and their combined experience lacks understanding and insight concerning the challenge at hand. Another issue may be defining the problem. Your eventual strategy may be focused on the wrong attributes and, as a result, the outcome will either be ineffective or counterproductive. Consider seeking an outside opinion to be the objective third party and new set of eyes on your problem. We are not promoting brand consultants here. The objective third party you eventually select may be a board member, industry expert, or personal mentor. Whomever you choose, make sure they are schooled in the practical application of strategy and are familiar enough with your industry, operation, and strengths and weaknesses.

In this manner, you can garner a sense of assurance that the brand triad process has been followed and a postmortem assessment will occur. We wish you the best as you apply this triad model to your unique situation. We welcome comments on this book, your experience with this technique, and any other comments you may have at www. BrandTriad.com. We will post your feedback and attempt to respond to all questions and comments.

REFERENCE LIST

1. Christensen, Clayton, Raynor, Michael. *The Innovator's Solution.* Harvard Business School Press, 2003.

2. The Wall Street Journal, *"Funds Add Fuel to Airline Deal Talk"* November 27, 2007, Corporate Focus Section, p.A8

3. The Wall Street Journal, *"Southwest's New Flight Plan: Win More Business Travelers"* November 27, 2007, Marketplace, p.B1

4. The Street.com, *"AMR to Spin Off Eagle"* November 28, 2007, http://www.thestreet.com/newsanalysis/transportation/10392063.html

5. Christensen, Clayton. *Seeing What's Next.* Harvard Business School Press, 2004.

6. The Wall Street Journal, *"When Fliers Avoid The Domestic Route"* November 27, 2007, Personal Journal Section, p.D1

7. Marketing Daily, *"Air Travelers Increasingly Dislike Having To Fly, Study Finds"* December 19, 2007, Internet E-mail, By Karl Greenberg

8. Kelly, Tom. *The Art of Innovation: Lessons in Creativity from IDEO, America's Leading Design Firm.* Doubleday, 2001.

9. CBS News, Interview with Howard Stringer, January 6, 2006, http://www.cbsnews.com/stories/2006/01/06/60minutes/main1183023.shtml

10. The Wall Street Journal, "Web Sites Want You to Stick Around" April 15, 2008, Business Technology Section, p.B5

11. CNN.COM, "Records: *Southwest Airlines flew 'unsafe' planes"* March 7, 2008, By Drew Griffin and Scott Bronstein, CNN Special Investigations Unit, **http://www.cnn.com/2008/US/03/06/southwest.planes/index.html**

12. Oxford University/Pepperdine University Program, *"Value Gap Analysis"* October 2003, Dr. Richard Schoenberg, http://www.som.cranfield.ac.uk/som/faculty/Showfaculty.asp?link=392

13. D'Aveni, Richard. *Hyper Competition: Managing the Dynamics of Strategic Maneuvering.* The Free Press, 1994

Chapter 4

Conclusion

As of April 2008, the challenges for the airline industry continue to mount. The headlines of the *Wall Street Journal* and many online news sites were almost daily reports of airlines going out of business, cancelling flights, and stranding passengers.

The Federal Aviation Administration, after the Southwest inspection mishap in March 2008, checked maintenance records on all domestic airlines. On April 9, 2008, American Airlines cancelled more than one thousand flights, which accounted for approximately one-third of their scheduled flights, due to an inspection of wiring on its fleet of 300 MD–80 jets. As reported by CNN on April 11, 2008, American Airlines CEO Gerard Arpey stated "I am profoundly sorry that we've gotten ourselves into this situation, and I thank our customers for their patience under very difficult circumstances." He acknowledged full responsibility for "failing to meet government inspection standards."

Gerard Arpe was also quoted as saying "the costs of the cancellations to American will run into the tens of millions of dollars, including vouchers to reimburse stranded customers, overtime for maintenance crews, and lost revenue." An analyst with Standard & Poor's estimated that it could easily top $30 million. On April 2, 2008, United Airlines cancelled thirty-one flights and grounded 11 percent of its fleet to test if a cargo fire suppression system was operating effectively. This action caused numerous cancellations and disrupted flight plans of more than one hundred forty thousand travelers.

Another *Wall Street Journal* article from April 8, 2008, discussed the ramifications of failed airlines and the effects on the traveling public. When Aloha Airlines, ATA Airlines, and Sky Bus closed their doors, one question remained: who will take their tickets?

What is happening with discount airlines? With the slowdown in the economy and $130 per barrel fuel prices, the idea of low fares is being challenged on every front. ATA Airlines filed for Chapter 11 bankruptcy, shut down its operations, and laid off two thousand two hundred employees. During the same week, Aloha Airgroup closed its doors and laid off one thousand nine hundred employees because it couldn't find capital or a buyer. A charter carrier called Champion Air suspended operations in May, affecting over five hundred jobs.

To offset higher fuel prices, many airlines are now charging higher ticket prices, surcharges for extra baggage, and booking fees. The balancing act they face continues to be competitive and covering incrementally rising expenses.

Another dynamic in the marketplace that was reported in late 2007 was talk of mergers. On April 22, 2008, Delta's CEO, Richard Anderson, announced the deal between Northwest and Delta that would form the world's largest airline. The apparent synergy described by Anderson suggests "by matching Delta's strengths on the East Coast, across the Atlantic, and to Latin America, with Northwest's presence in the Midwest and across the Pacific, the two airlines make up what each lacks individually." The challenge now facing Anderson and his deal lies in the hands of antitrust officials at the state department and shareholders of both airlines.

The interesting part of industry consolidation seems to mask the real problem. By combining similar enterprises doesn't address the real issue: rising costs! Merging two organizations is challenging enough (cultures, equipment, process, etc.) and could take much more effort (time, money, resources) to effectively align the new business. How does this transaction meet the goals of both the traveling public and operational efficiency?

Based on the information presented, it seems the domestic market will fall to those organizations that can deliver on customer needs in the most effective manner. Larger, more complex organizations don't possess the ability to deliver that type of value. Over time, the larger companies can't afford to play in the market and will focus on transcontinental and international routes instead. After winning the domestic battle, the next obvious up-market move the domestic winner will take will be international. This natural phenomenon has already transpired in the automotive marketplace. Toyota was once the small disrupter who focused on the low end of the market. Next, they moved up-market to full size and luxury models. Now, like Southwest did with airlines, they have redefined the automotive market with hybrid technology and are leading this category.

The common thread in all industries, whether automotive, airline, hotel, or mobile music. is who can deliver a value proposition that meets the needs of a consuming public. Although that statement seems overly simplistic, billions of dollars are being lost year after year, and companies are filing bankruptcy or being sold for peanuts. What happened along the way, and what strategy was employed? A postmortem root-cause analysis could be undertaken to understand, but what predictive tool are these firms using to avert disaster?

Challenges Facing Your Business

Let's close out this section by considering your particular business issue. What challenge does your organization currently face? Are you experiencing a general slowdown in certain target markets, or do you find customers (B2B) are delaying purchases? If you sell to consumers, does your offering solve a problem that is unaffected by the current economic outlook or, conversely, subjected to it? How will you determine the gaps in the marketplace that are presently not being addressed? These and many more issues affect your business on a daily basis and require a process to uncover and assess baseline assumptions.

There are many approaches to analyzing your value proposition with respect to the markets you serve. You can assess sales trends and compare them to industry economic statistics. Close correlations naturally occur between markets and business prosperity. If you sold critical components in the defense industry during a government build-up, you would naturally enjoy those revenues. However, if you didn't diversify into other markets, a defense spending slowdown would greatly impact your business and lead to downsizing. If you're a consumer-based business, understanding leading edge trends will help you adjust your strategy in advance of these impending changes. Whether these changes take the form of a global economic event, such as gas prices, or cultural changes, such as the emergence of generation X and Y influence, monitoring and modifying your business strategy on a daily basis has now become the norm.

The brand triad model serves many functions in addition to managing your future brand trajectory. Foremost, it centers on your business strategy by evaluating what business you are in and the audience(s) you currently serve. This situational analysis goes beyond numbers and attempts to assess the psychology of consumer behavior as it pertains to your products and services and constituency. Only by understanding the daily problems that need to be solved by your customers can you begin the process of understanding the true value you deliver to the marketplace. With this understanding in hand, you may then better align your business to the markets you serve.

Once you can clearly delineate what your customer needs and what you currently offer then gaps suddenly emerge. These adjacent opportunities that surround your current product or service may or may not require you to adjust aspects of your brand identity. As illustrated in the airline gap analysis, you may need to increase, reduce, or eliminate certain attributes of your offering to take advantage of these opportunities. As you make these adjustments, you will need to continually monitor consumer responses to these changes. Keeping your fingers on the pulse of your business and reactions to your product or service mix will be crucial.

Another important outcome of utilizing the brand triad model is the distribution of customer responses. These can be both quantitative and qualitative in nature. The raw numbers will provide a historic view of past events and possible trend lines leading to the future. On the other hand, qualitative data provides a glimpse behind the curtain and is telling of how customers view both past and current behavior. But is this enough?

We believe the answer is no. We suggested that the use of observers may help to uncover actual customer behavior. As previously mentioned, surveys may not be as reliable because customers tend to either be complimentary or something less than honest when asked their opinion. In addition, customers don't possess the vocabulary to describe what they really want or need. If you interviewed consumers pertaining to a next generation CD player, they would not arrive at the iPod or some other derivative. They would simply ask for a less expensive, vibration resistant, and more compact player. Attributes such as random access, one thousand song storage capabilities, iTunes library, and other amenities would not be on the forefront of their minds. In effect, you are asking too much of your customers to provide your next generation product or service. Also, if you do place stock in what they request, you'll find yourself creating an offering that no one truly wants or needs. Observing your clientele clearly illuminates two things: struggles they are having with your products or services and improvements that are necessary.

We also suggested that consumers buy products and services on their terms and during a time that's convenient for them. Our responsibility as business owners is to understand the habits of these users and provide opportunities to engage our brands. Using the hotel scenario from chapter one, take advantage of a connection that was initiated by an interested consumer as it is your optimal engagement point. They are seeking your products and services and are, at that juncture, most open to some minor questions. If these mini invasions are viewed as helpful and beneficial, the consumer will be willing to invest for his or her greater benefit. Offering adjacent opportunities to your core brand accomplishes two objectives: providing the customer or consumer with more closely related amenities, such as a greater share of wallet, and shifting their perception from casual to preferred user. During each subsequent touch point, these users build upon previous engagements by customizing their experience. Options such as "my favorites" or a configuration tool such as room amenities for hotels pass control to the user and allows them to design their future experience. Soon your casual user becomes an advocate for your brand. If the engagement becomes ingrained in their lives and a dependency occurs, they may become your best form of promotion because they will adorn themselves with your company's image and proudly wear it as a badge of honor. This, of course, is the goal of a great brand!

Another important activity your business may want to engage in is listening. How do you garner feedback from your employees, customers, and stakeholders? There are many ways vital information is passed along that could help your business thrive and be attuned to changes in the marketplace. Consider listening inside your organization.

Clayton Christensen created an interesting model that deals with the decision making process within a company. One path is deliberate, and the other is emergent. Senior managers generally deliver the deliberate objectives to the organization in forms such as strategic and tactical plans. A good example might be a small nonprofit that produces cotton and wool sweaters for the homeless. The leaders in the organization may determine the number of cotton sweaters for the year and organize the activities around a certain production output. At the same time, the demand for wool sweaters increases due to an early winter. The organization naturally adapts to the change and shifts production away from cotton and focuses on wool. Despite the planning methods employed by senior managers, this organization adapted to the climatic changes and, thus, reorganized around relevant requirements. This example demonstrates an organization that listens and adapts to the needs of the marketplace.

From a customer perspective, the use of blogs, forums, and survey tools may help acquire the necessary feedback on your company and offerings in the marketplace. As mentioned in chapter three, Southwest Airlines used their blog to deal with a maintenance safety issue and provided a venue for all to vent and comment on Southwest's actions. Monitoring your blog and other related forums will help you understand what your constituency is saying about you, and it allows you the opportunity to set the record straight. There are numerous examples of firms that headed off disaster by joining the conversation online and providing objectivity in order to counter subjective claims.

The primary function of the triad model comes in the form of positioning your business. Once you determine your current state, senior management can begin the process of assessing possible strategies and subsequent risks and rewards associated with each move. By considering attributes, behavior, and circumstances, management can view the full spectrum of opportunities and possible outcomes that surround your brand and business. During scenario planning, the management team can manipulate this model on all three continuums and determine the cost in time, money, and resources to achieve such changes. In some cases, augmenting movements along each leg may not be possible because they lie outside the realm of control by the firm. Understanding these limitations will inject a dose of reality into the strategic planning process and help senior managers avoid unpleasant surprises in the future.

By digging deeper into each of the continuums, the organization can now move into the second dimension, which is a precursor and view of things to come. This, by no means, is a magic eight ball that will uncover every ailment that plagues your market space or business, but it does serve as an early warning system for your ongoing concern. As noted in the hotel example, developing insight and discernment into the behavior of your constituency will help unmask the subtleties that may affect the future of your core business. Understanding the prevailing aggregate beliefs and tone of your customer base will help you develop a trajectory of future behavior. With this information in hand, senior managers may adjust the value proposition and test this concept in a local market. The process of constantly testing such hypotheses enables management to learn and develop new sets of values that will help retain valuable patrons.

Once you have plotted the second dimension for each continuum, you can step back from the data and assess changes over time. After each minor adjustment has been implemented, you can visually monitor the resultant shifts that are underway and determine the net effect, albeit positive or negative. For example, if your hotel quickly matches the amenities (fast follower) of the new hotel, the change on the second dimension may be reduced, neutralized, or cause a return to the original position. The aggregate consensus of patrons may be to stay with your current offering because competitive amenities have been matched. The rating along the second dimension might even increase because the consumer achieves greater benefits without making a painful change.

Even if you miss the signals on the second dimension and now witness a change along the main continuum, all is not lost. By examining the data, you may quickly discern those areas that attributed to a disruption and, thus, focus on changing key amenities. The salient point here is to monitor shifts in customer and consumer behavior. It was once said that it costs seven times more to find a new client than to keep your current patron happy. In turn, it is more painful to find new vendors, partnerships, alliances, and brands than to stay with what we know. Change is hard and we all avoid it as much as possible.

Summation

In closing, the primary benefit of the brand triad model is that of a strategic assessment and repositioning tool for business managers and marketers alike. This is, by no means, a silver bullet axiom for all business ailments. The real value lies in the discovery and recognition process to uncover your brand's current state. In a world that moves at breakneck speeds, parsing out time to step back and take stock of your business and future direction is not only important but also healthy.

The creation of the brand triad model was not some revolutionary idea that changes traditional business analysis or nullifies marketing paradigms as we know it. If anything, its basis is rather commonsense and enables the mapping of a business trajectory. The conceptual idea was derived several years go on a rather long drive from Orlando to Hialeah, Florida with a sales professional. The topic of favorite beverages came up during our conversation, and my associate named Starbucks cappuccino as a daily "must have." Being naturally curious, I began to inquire as to his thought process and rationale behind his brand dependency.

He began with all the attributes of the Starbucks brand and drew comparisons between that and less desirable offerings. This included temperature, taste, content, mixture, and even the shape and style of the paper cup. Because he spent his life on the road, the actual interior of Starbucks was of little consequence to him, and he valued locations that possessed a drive-through. Those are the attributes: product, places, and things.

He then went on to discuss his behavior as it relates to this brand. This was the easy part. He would rather forego the effort to get off the freeway—he puts fifty thousand miles on his business vehicle per year—than to substitute his preferred brand for some adjacent or periphery offering.

Finally, I wanted to understand how far he would travel to find a Starbucks store. As we drove down the highway, I pointed to an exit. "Would you stop if you saw a Starbucks sign from the freeway?" I asked. "Of course," he quickly replied. "What if the store was one block from the exit?" He rubbed his chin as if deep in thought and then blurted out "Sure!" Not to press the point, but my curiosity got the better of me. "Two blocks?" He turned and gave me a look as if to say *you've got to be kidding me.* "Yes," he said with a terse smile. "One mile?" I asked. At this point, he was growing tired of the inquisition and closed out the discussion with "no more than one mile from the off-ramp, and that's my final answer."

As I thought about our conversation as we cruised down Highway 95, it became clear to me that a real dialogue transpires as we consider which brands we'll choose and the circumstances surrounding those purchases. What if we could capture this dialogue during the search and decision making process? Although it is not practical to record every consumer's thought process, there must be a method for capturing at least a portion of the brand selection and, subsequently, making use of this information in aggregate.

"Thought-bites"

After reading this book, you can tell I'm an advocate of utilizing both the web site and customer engagement points to garner this consumer dialogue. It's true that capturing a consensus stream of thought is not possible, but building upon "thought-bites" is very practical and achievable. The other important aspect of a collection of data over time allows the marketer to make adjustments based on changes to the value proposition. By tracking responses to new programs or offerings, an almost real-time feedback will allow you to adjust your brand model.

Once the brand triad model has been constructed, infusing new data from scattergrams at regular intervals, such as a quarterly basis, will help paint a picture of both subtle and significant movements. Depending on your business model and offering, it might be practical to employ observers on an annual basis to ensure integrity of the data. At the same time, observers may find new opportunities or gaps that may be emerging in your market space. The key is to continuously monitor your market(s) and business.

One final note: The process of applying the brand triad model over time will yield new insights and adaptations to the overall concept. Not unlike software or other consumables, constant refinement of the approach and new mechanisms will most certainly be created and added to this model. Working in concert with a variety of firms in diverse industries will illuminate the complexities and challenges associated with a one-size-fits-all standard model. It seems reasonable that derivations of this basic concept will be created to address specific markets, scenarios, and business model types.

As previously mentioned, a blog has been established to enlist your thoughts about this book, concerns or questions about this theory, and experiences in practical application. Your insights and use of this model will only help to further develop and refine this assessment tool and process. We gladly welcome your thoughts at www.BrandTriad. com.